THE MESSAGE OF
THE DIVINE ILIAD

THE MESSAGE OF
THE DIVINE ILIAD

WALTER RUSSELL

VOLUME I

LIMITED

Edition De Luxe

UNIVERSITY OF SCIENCE AND PHILOSOPHY
FORMERLY THE WALTER RUSSELL FOUNDATION
SWANNANOA, WAYNESBORO, VIRGINIA 22980

Printed in Canada
Jacket & Drawings by Author

FOREWORD

THE MESSAGE OF THE DIVINE ILIAD is sent from our Father to give unfolding humanity the needed comprehension for taking the next transforming step in man's long journey from the jungle of sensed awareness of body to cosmic conscious awareness of omnipresent Light of God as the centering motivating force of man.

For millions of years, man was unaware of his conscious Self. He was but body, expressing the desires of body, constantly seeking that which his body needed, and taking it by his might of physical strength. During those æons of his unfolding, man was totally unaware of his unity with God and mankind. Likewise, he was totally unaware of the universal inexorable law which governed his every action.

Then came the dawn of Consciousness. Man began to *know*. Then he created extensions of his body to do for him what his body could not do. He created a boat to transport his body—then a sail for the boat

—then a wheel—and fire to warm him and cook *the food which he* formerly ate raw during the animal stage of his unfolding.

Then came the long savage and barbarian stages of increasingly complex human relations based upon the jungle principle of taking that which he wanted by the power of might-over-right. During thousands of years tribes warred upon other tribes, building themselves into nations, and then empires, to gain possession of the wealth and services of other tribes and nations by acquiring their lands and people for ownership and exploitation.

Our own United States were thus acquired. We killed without compunction to obtain what we wanted. We stole hundreds of thousands of negroes and made slaves of them. England, France, The Netherlands, Russia and other nations multiplied their empires by the sword of the mighty slaying the weak.

Industrial empires came into being as our supposedly highly civilized and enlightened society of humans increased its knowledge and practice of the arts and sciences. Advancement in our cultures and standard of living continued to deceive us as to our status as civilized beings. We failed to realize that we were illegitimately *still practicing the law of the jungle*—which takes only what it needs for survival

—while man took thousands of times more than he needed for material gain. The jungle kills one at a time for food, but man kills by millions for enslavement and exploitation.

Such practices are a normal part of our present standard of civilization. It is difficult to realize that we are still barbarians. A civilization which kills and exploits others for mere gain can hardly call itself *civilized*. Humans can never justly call themselves civilized until they practice the love principle which God practices in all of His Creation.

Mankind has reached that stage of his unfolding where he must either learn the facts of inexorable universal law and practice them, or perish by his own hand. He will die by the sword he slays with unless his entire human relations are reversed from the taking principle to Nature's principle of balanced giving for regiving.

Man's scientific skills have made it possible for him to slay his entire race. A continuation of the old *barbarian practice of taking,* which has bred his many wars of hatred and aggression, will inevitably lead to a war of extinction unless *Nature's love principle of giving* replaces it.

Today the world is divided. Disunity marks all human relations—from industry to religion—from capital to labor. Two opposing world ideologies—

democracy and communism—stand like insurmountable precipices to debar world unity. Freedom itself is not two centuries old. Slavery was existent in our own country within the memory of living men. Through ignorance and superstition, America's colonial intellectuals burned old women at the stake as witches. Mighty empires are still attempting to build themselves into greater empires by the sword.

Man is at the crossroads of his unfolding. The old way of life which built his empires of hate and fear *must* be abandoned. This coming age must be built upon God's one law of balanced interchange in all human relations. There is no other alternative. To continue the old way means the destruction of civilization by multiplied hate. To follow the new path will mean the multiplication of love which *alone* will bring peace, happiness and prosperity to man.

Man's comprehension has been limited to the range of his senses. Man is now unfolding beyond the range of material sensing in the direction of *cosmic knowing.* Science is doing this for him. Science is slowly, but surely, verifying the personal God of man's demanding and identifying the invisible, spiritual Personal Being of man with the invisible, spiritual Personal Being of God.

Science is thus replacing man's abstract god of faith and belief with a dynamic God of law and order

Whom man KNOWS. The abstract god of faith and belief is the direct cause of man's many religions, for abstractions have bred many concepts of God, where knowledge can conceive but the ONE. Faith and belief are the shield of ignorance.

THE MESSAGE OF THE DIVINE ILIAD is to build a scientific comprehension of the nature of God—and man's unity with God—in order that mankind may unfold in the direction of its ultimate goal of cosmic awareness of the Light rather than refold by descending into the terrors of another deep and long dark age.

Through love alone can man find the kingdom of heaven for which he has sought since his beginnings. Only through *living love* as a principle can he find the happiness, peace and prosperity which lie in his heart as the greatest of his desires.

God is the Light of all-knowing. Creation is a thought-wave universe which records God's knowing as expressed by God's electric thinking.

THE DIVINE ILIAD cannot be fully published for many years. The first excerpts from it were published in *THE SECRET OF LIGHT*. As much more of it as can now be published will appear in this volume. Further portions of it will be released in accordance with instructions specifically given for their release in *THE DIVINE ILIAD*.

WALTER RUSSELL

TABLE OF CONTENTS

PART I

SIX CHAPTERS FROM
THE DIVINE ILIAD

THE BOOK OF DESIRE

A Communion

1. I am in the kingdom of Thy heavens, O my Father-Mother. Speak Thou to me lest my words to man be but my words, not Thine and mine.

2. Earth is far. I behold it not, know it not. I but sense it afar through flux threads which bind me to it lightly.

3. I know Thee only in me; Thee, the Light of my Self. Thee, the two lights of my far body which lies enfolded in Thy body awaiting Self of it, Self of me, Self of Thee at its reborning.

4. Deep upon my heart are questionings which I must answer in words, for which there are no words.

5. Intent am I upon the pulse-beat of Thy thinking, O my Father.

6. Extend Thou the two interweaving lights of Thy thinking to my Consciousness that my knowing shall rightly interpret Thy thinking through the pulse-beat of my thinking.

THE WORD

I

1. *"Write thou these words for men.*

2. *"Through My messengers I have told man to cast his bread upon the waters and it would return to him multiplied, but he comprehendeth it not e'en to this day.*

3. *"Through My messengers I have told man that it is not easy for him who loveth riches of earth alone to enter My kingdom, but he still fails to comprehend that he may have great riches and still find his way to Me, through obeying My One Law.*

4. *"Write thou My law for him a hundred times, yea a hundred times a hundred times, and exemplify it unceasingly, that he may know it inviolate, that he may know it irrevocable, and that he may find ecstasy in obeying it."*

II

1. *"Write thou again My oft said words: 'Desire ye what ye will and it shall be thine. All My universe will give it thee in the strength of thy desiring and in the strength of thy action in reaching out for thy desire.'*

2. *"Heed ye thy desires lest they be unlawful.*

2

Measure ye thy desires carefully against their opposites, lest unbalanced desires breed their unbalanced kind to arise and smite thee.

3. *"For again I say My one principle of My one law is founded upon the solid rock of equal interchange between all pairs of opposite things, opposite conditions or opposite transactions between men.*

4. *"My will must prevail on earth as it is in heaven. That which I divide to give to earths and their surrounding heavens of space is equal.*

5. *"That which earths give to their surrounding space balances that which space gives to earths.*

6. *"See thou My will thus working irrevocably in the starry systems which constitute My immortal, eternal body.*

7. *"Note thou the precision of earth paths through their heavens. Know thou that such precision is result of obedience to My will which My law is.*

8. *"Tell thou these workings of My law in the firmament of My body to man who knows those workings but denies Me in them.*

9. *"Tell man My rhythms are absolute, else the interlacing of earth paths through their heavens could not be. Tell him also that chaos must arise from his unbalanced comings and goings, his givings and takings, e'en as chaos would arise from disobedience*

3

*to My will in the comings and goings of earth paths
through their heavens, or the givings and re-givings
of their interchanging pressures.*

*10. "When skies take of earth unequally with
earth's taking of the skies, tornadoes tell both earth
and skies that I am within and without them, yea
within and without every particle of them, and theirs
is the agony of disobedience to My will.*

*11. "Not till they obey My will do they find
peace and rest in My tranquillity.*

*12. "These do I balance with My will as I bal-
ance all divided pairs in My universe of Me.*

*13. "Likewise, when man takes aught from earth
and gives naught to Me for regiving through Self of
him, toxins arise within him which are tornadoes for
his self quelling."*

III

*1. "Say thou to men: ye are My body. Hear thou
Me when I say that thy desires are thy Selves, yea
both body and Spirit of Thee.*

*2. "That which thou would'st possess is Thee,
e'en though thou possess it not. In body it is Thee.
In patterned Seed and Soul it is Thee. That thou
canst not evade. Thou, thy Self, create thy Self in
thy image.*

3. "If thou desirest gold of earth without balanc-

4

THE BOOK OF DESIRE

ing thy taking of it by giving gold of heaven in equal measure thy very Soul records the changing of thy unbalanced Soul pattern to the measure of thy unbalancing.

4. "He who discords the patterns of My balanced will discords his very seed. Its rhythms he must make absolute e'en as the disturbed rhythms of earth's storms must be made absolute. From this, My decree, there is no escape for man, nor star, nor galaxy in My universe which I imagined into seeming being to manifest Me.

5. "Balance thy desires and they will bless thee with multiples of their kind. Beware lest thy taking shall outweigh thy giving and gain thee naught."

IV

1. "Consider well My will. Disregard it not, for thou shalt well pay heavily for e'en one whit of its breaching.

2. "For I am balance. As heavens and earths of My balanced radial body vary not one whit in their rhythmic balance, so shall man vary not one whit.

3. "Unknowing man unthinkingly counts upon his own power to set aside My one law to fit the measure of his desires, but, I say, I alone hold balance.

4. "Man walks through his cycles upon a tautened

*rope. Where'er his foot toucheth I am there, giving
him foothold as the fulcrum of his effort.*

*5. "From My rest at that fulcrum he takes the
power I give to him to express his desire. Without
Me he can do naught.*

*6. "And behold Me also at each end of the lever
of his action to balance his unbalancing in My universe which knows no unbalance.*

*7. "Yea, be it ever known that two eyes of man's
very God watch o'er each action of each man whose
body My body is.*

*8. "And if man would know where those two
eyes of his God are located, I say seek them at each
end of his wavering pole which keeps him upright
upon his tautened rope.*

*9. "For man cannot be without Me e'en though
he deny Me in him.*

*10. "Have a care, therefore, that desires of man
for things of earth be balanced by desires for heavenly blessings, without which man has naught."*

V

*1. "Know thou, My messenger, that I, thy God,
ruleth o'er all things of My imagining.*

*2. "For I am absolute, and all things which ex-
tendeth from the Light of My imagining are absolute.*

6

3. "Likewise I am perfection, as I am Truth. All things which extendeth from me are perfect. They are Truth.

4. "That which seems imperfect to man's eyes is but seeming, for he sees not all. Could he see all he would see all perfect.

5. "As the unfinished picture seems imperfect in man's eyes, for it is not the whole, it is perfect could he see the whole.

6. "Likewise each brush-stroke of a concept is perfect for that stage of its unfolding.

7. "Likewise each stage of man's unfolding is a perfect part of the whole idea of man's unfolding. There is no evil in it. Nor is there imperfection anywhere. There is but the One Whole of everything in Me, and all is perfect, all is absolute.

8. "For My universe is but the forever unfolding-refolding of My One Whole Idea. As My Whole Idea is perfect so, also, is each part perfect.

9. "For I watch o'er all borning things until their rebirth in Me. At their birth in Me their perfection is My perfection. Likewise, at their rebirth in Me their perfection is their inheritance from Me.

10. "At each stage of their unfolding and refolding they are absolute and perfect, for I am absolute and perfect.

11. "That which man lacks in his knowing is still

7

his in Me, awaiting his desire for knowing. When he desires to know he may know.

12. "Likewise that which man seemingly unbalances in his actions is balanced in Me awaiting his balancing. And that day will come, for man cannot evade that day.

13. "Unbalance and imperfection exist not, therefore, save in man's timed seeing. For him who knows My Light there is no timed seeing.

14. "Desire of man, or tree, or earth, or giant nebula is balanced in Me always. Unbalance exists not in My house. Imperfection and untruth, likewise, exist not in My house. Likewise error and evil exist not in My house.

15. "These are but each end of man's balance pole upon which he walks waveringly through his cycles, knowing not that I am there measuring his unbalancing to void it at the other end with equal opposed measure.

16. "For I balance all things as they occur by voiding all things as they occur, for, hark thou Me as I again say that all My universe is but My imaginings; and I am not My imaginings.

17. "Thus do I watch o'er earths which desire extensions of their paths to outer reaches farther from their mother suns. Two eyes have I to watch o'er each of these, two eyes to balance each with each, and two to balance each with every other thing that is.

18. "And, likewise, when earths give birth to moons, two eyes have I for these two also, two eyes to measure paths for them which balance with paths of all things else in the universe.

19. "And, likewise, when earth mothers men, and other extensions of My life, to pulse My pulse of life and live in Me, two eyes have I for each countless part of them, to watch o'er each separate part, to keep it one with all My universe.

20. "Not the veriest microcosm in all My electric body which is not thus double poled, within and without, by My two watchful eyes.

21. "No path of man, or bird, or creeping thing, lies unmeasured and unwatched by Me.

22. "All paths of all things in My radial body are but one path, for, of a verity I say, that slightest move of creeping thing on this small earth is recorded upon all paths of all things, e'en to giant star beyond man's seeing.

23. "Thus do I control all desires of all things which manifest My One Idea. Likewise I see to it that all their happenings which man calls bad, or good, or error, or evil, add up to the zero of balance in Me. For there is naught in My universe which can be added to, or subtracted from, which is more or less than the zero from which all things spring into their seeming being, to end where they began for re-beginning.

24. *"Hear Me again say there are not two halves of a divided one in all the pairs of opposites of My universe. There are but a seeming two, and each one of these is of the other one while seeming to be two. And each becomes the other one sequentially to maintain that seeming.*

25. *"There is naught upon the earth which comes not from the heavens. Likewise there is naught within the heavens which comes not from their centering earths and suns.*

26. *"Each quickens the other with the giving of each to each equally for each other's equal re-giving.*

27. *"Again I say that equal interchange is My will. He who desires aught in My Cosmos must obey My will. He who so obeys My will commands My will to fruition of his desire."*

VI

1. *"Hearken to My word when I say that desires of man are patterned seed which repeat their kind. That pattern which man fashions into seed of his desire will multiply in like form for his reaping.*

2. *"And the reaping will be as sure as that the dawn cometh to him unasked by him. For man is*

what his desire is. His image is the pattern of his thinking.

3. *"Observe ye all men My one inviolate law of rhythmic balanced interchange in all thy thinking, and in all thy dealing. Happiness, or anguish, will be thine in the measure of its observance.*

4. *"Should ye desire to kill, the whole power of My universe will help ye kill; but by the sword ye killeth with shall ye also be killed.*

5. *"Likewise My law will give all power to aid him who would bless another by a kindly act. He who so desires to bless shall reap blessings from seed of that desire multiplied a hundred times.*

6. *"A humble act done unperceived in My name will open wide the door of My kingdom for him who doeth right action for right action's sake alone; but he who doeth mighty things for self glory shall not know My Light.*

7. *"Desire for thus acting, thus manifesting Me, is manifoldly blessed, but he who maketh loud protestations for the same act does it not in My name but in his own, denying Me in him.*

8. *"Verily, I say, he who giveth in My name storeth up great riches in the rhythms of heaven which are as immortal as the Soul-seed of his Self is immortal.*

9. *"But he who taketh riches in his own name,*

giving naught of his Self to Me to void the greed of his self-taking, gathers naught to himself but riches which are as mortal as the clay of his earth self is mortal.

10. "Things alone of earth which man desires are but things of earth to be returned to earth with bones of him. But things of earth, heaven blessed by Me, are as eternal in the immortality of his Self recording Soul as Light of Me is eternal.

11. "He who desireth riches of earth alone, denying Me in him, shall dwell in outer darkness of his own making until he shall desire Me strongly.

12. "E'en to him will I give all he asketh without stinting, yea, and even more; but he, having more than all he sought will have naught but worthless dross of his earth desire.

13. "And darkness will enshroud him. No Light will there be in his eyes, nor will he know love. Having desired the dark without My Light, he will have but acquired the dark.

14. "He who desireth peace on earth must find it in heaven.

15. "Therefore, I say, he who desireth aught through Me shall have his desire throughout eternity, for it shall be written in his recording Soul in lines of Light, but he who gaineth riches of earth alone, with lack of Me in them, writeth black lines upon his eternal Soul which he must whiten through long ages of undoing.

16. "For, I say, there are two opposed ways in the journey of man from his jungle to his mountain top. One leads backward to the blackness of his primal jungle. The other way leads to Me.

17. "Man may choose his way, for man's purpose in manifesting Me is to find his way out of the dark to Light of Me throughout long ages of new knowing through repeated action.

18. "He who walks toward the Light through right action writes new lines of Light upon his Soul; but he who walks toward the dark takes on the dark, and no Light is there in him.

19. "Hear thou Me when I say that man writes his own record of his thinking, and his acting, in his own immortal Soul; and that which man writes there will be repeated in the patterned seed of the reborning of that man unto eternity.

20. "Some far day he will come to Me to find rest, but until that day of knowing Me in him he shall walk the treadmill of earth unceasingly.

21. "There are those among men of earth who deem desire unholy. These seek holiness, and Me, through the suppression of all desires.

22. "These sit in quietude, seeking Me through meditation, but acting not to manifest My purpose.

*Yet these ask alms, in My name, of those who fulfill
My purpose through thought followed by action.*

23. *"I command thee to tell to these misguided
holy men, who sell their holiness for a price to those
who unknowingly buy naught of holiness for their
wasted gold, that they who thus sit begging by the
road in mortifying rags shall never find Me whom
they seek, until they act to fulfill My purpose.*

24. *"Tell thou them that they are as unclean in
thy Father-Mother's eyes as the stench of them is
unwholesome to men of earth.*

25. *"Said I not these very words in the beginning
of thy full knowing Me in thee: 'Desire is of the
Soul, the Soul being record of desire fulfilled by action for repeating its pattern in the seed?'*

26. *"And also said I not to thee: 'My creating
universe is the continuing record of My eternal
thinking, followed by action to record the patterned
imaged forms of My thinking?'*

27. *"And again said I not to thee: 'My sole desire
is to think for the purpose of expressing the One Idea
of My thinking through imaged forms of My imagining engaged in purposeful action?'*

28. *"And also have I not said: 'My Cosmos of the
divided lights of My thinking which is recorded by
the making of My earths and heavens, and all My
children of the earths and heavens all made in My*

image, is My body, centered by the Light of Me, created by desire in Me to manifest desire in Me?'

29. *"Hear thou Me when I again say that My recorded universe is purposeful. It is idea expressed through action. It is not just idea in thought alone, being never writ through the inter-action of the interweaving lights of My thinking.*

30. *"Wherefore, say I, there would be no universe were My thinking not recorded by the action of My extended lights of desire in Me.*

31. *"If these useless beggars by the road think themselves holy for the suppression of desire to fulfill My purpose by actions which fulfill My purpose, then am I, their One God, unholy for desiring them to fulfill My purpose.*

32. *"Again, and yet again, shalt thou, My messenger, write down these, My Words, and say them unto all men.*

33. *"Desire ye what ye will, and behold, it standeth before thee. Throughout the aeons it has been thine without thy knowing, e'en though thou hast but just asked for it.*

34. *"Sit thou not and ask, acting not, for unless thou reach out for thy desire it shall not walk thy way to thee, unaided by thy strong arms.*

35. *"Behold I am within all things, centering them. And I am without all things, controlling them.*

But I am not those things which I center and control.

36. "I am the center of My universe of Me. Everywhere I am is the center of all things, and I am everywhere."

Thus saith the Universal One, Father-Mother of the heavens and earths, and all His children of the heavens and earths, to me upon the mountain top, in waves of the two lights of His thinking.

THE BOOK OF REST

A Communion

1. I am in the Light.
2. I know the Light.
3. I am in the Spirit.
4. The doors of dimension have closed upon my body and shown me to be a living Light shining out of the darkness.
5. I know the Source of things beyond the extensions of things.
6. I am One with the essence of things beyond the motion of things.
7. I know my oneness with the One.
8. God abideth in me. I know that I am He. I know God's kingdom of the Light.
9. I know my universality.
10. The Consciousness of space is mine.
11. The Light of God's equilibrium is my guide. I know its balance, unextended, undivided. Out of its essence comes the Word and the Law to counsel me.
12. The language of Light is mine to know.
13. All that is, is Light.

14. Thou, my Father-Mother, hast commanded that I write down in words for man the meaning within Thy Light which is written upon my heart in waves of Thy inspired essence of meaning which I must interpret into man's words.

15. Guide Thou me, Thou Source of me, as I write words which shall be truly Thine, not mine alone, nor e'en Thine and mine.

THE WORD

I

1. "I am the Knower of the Known.

2. "I am the sexless Knower of the Known. In Me is the Consciousness of all-knowing. And that is My power.

3. "In Me, the unconditioned One, is the Whole. There are no parts, nor are there beginnings, nor endings in Me, the One Conscious Whole.

4. "I am the dual Thinker of unfolding parts of the Known, the Imaginer of imaged forms which emerge from My knowing, through My thinking, to manifest My knowing.

5. "My dual thinking divides My knowing Light into pairs of sex-divided mirrors of the two opposed lights of My thinking. These electric mirrors of divided light reflect My Light and Life in them for manifesting My knowing and the One Life of My

18

Being. Forever and forever they interchange the dual reflected lights of My thinking for manifesting the continuance of My thinking, yet they are not My Light, nor are they My Life.

6. "Nor are they My Being. I, My all-conscious Being alone live, and I alone think.

7. "Again I say, all thinking is My thinking. Also I say, when man thinks at all he thinks with Me as One, imagines with Me as One, and builds his images with Me as One.

8. "And when man is inspired by exalted thinking know thou that it is I in him who am thinking as One with him.

9. "For I am the Source of ecstasy and inspiration in man. Behold in Me the Silent Voice which man may hear who hath inner ears to hear. And I am the Light which man may see who hath eyes of the Spirit to see.

10. "For I say that in-so-far as man knows the ecstasy of inspiration in him he hears My Voice and sees My Light in him. He then knows the mighty rhythms of My balanced thinking and thinks with Me."

II

1. "Come unto Me in My high heavens, ye who are burdened of earth, and find rest.

2. "For I am Rest; and I am Love, and all the

19

unchanging qualities which My thinking divides into paired quantities of sex-conditioned extensions of My Light which ever seek the rest in Me from which they sprang.

3. "And never do they find rest while unaware of Me in them, for they are but moving images of My imaginings which forever move as sexed extensions of the sexless Light from which they sprang.

4. "For moving things of clay forever move, knowing not that rest centers their moving as rest centers the shaft which forever moves around its very Source of rest, from which its motion springs.

5. "Knowing not Me, their Source of Rest in them, they cannot be that Source around which they must forever move to seek that which they cannot find until they know Me in them.

6. "Knowing not Me in them, they are alone in all the universe; but knowing Self of them as Me in them, they then are Me; they then, with Me, are all My universe.

7. "Verily, I say, the power of moving things to move, or to find rest, is not in them. I, alone, am energy; and I am also rest.

8. "I am the fulcrum which extends the power to move from rest.

9. "Thine arm is not empowered to pulse alone, unextended from the rest-point in thine heart; nor is one microscopic thing empowered to manifest Me apart from Me."

III

1. "*My rest and peace may be known by moving things which know My balance in them and keep balance in them while thus moving.*

2. "*Moving things which manifest My knowing by equal interchanging void their moving and thus find rest;—but those which manifest Me unequally cannot wholly void their moving.*

3. "*These shall leave an unvoided residue of motion as a debt of unbalance which must be paid to Me before My rest may be known in them.*

4. "*For I am Balance; and all moving things which extend from Me must manifest My balance in them. And I am Law. No rest can there be, nor can there be peace, while My law remains broken by unbalance e'en by one whit.*

5. "*For verily I give rest to moving things by equally dividing Light of My knowing at rest in Me to extending and retracting lights of My thinking. Know thou that as My knowing is balanced and at rest in Me so is My thinking balanced and at rest in Me.*

6. "*The extending light of My thinking multiplies the oneness of My knowing into many ones to*

mother them as formed bodies made in patterned images of My knowing.

7. "The retracting light gathers all the many ones together into My oneness to father them in Soul-seed of Me for again borning into patterned forms of many ones.

8. "In this wise My formless knowing is imaged in many patterned moving forms which seek rest from moving in the formlessness of My unity for reborning as many patterned moving forms.

9. "For I am Rest. In My rest is My knowing. From My rest extends My balanced electric thinking. In action and reaction of My thinking I am balanced always;—for I am Balance, as I am also Rest.

10. "When man's thinking is balanced in him as it is in Me then shall he know rest in Me as I know rest in Me. Then shall his thinking be the ecstasy of his knowing, as My thinking is the ecstasy of My knowing.

11. "Know thou that Mind of Me is ecstatic always. I know neither grief nor pain, sorrow nor compassion, anger nor wrath, for these are qualities of unbalance, and unbalance is not in My house. Know thou that these unbalanced qualities are product of man's unbalanced thinking. They alone are in him. They are not in Me."

IV

1. "He who knows not Me in him first thinks himself as one of many separate and separable forms apart from all things else, and Me. In those, his early days, he knows not Me in him, not suspecting Me in him, e'en though his slightest move is Mine; yea e'en though his very breathing is desire in Me that he should breathe to manifest Me in him, though unknowingly.

2. "Man then knows not himself as one of seeming many forms of My imagining which spring from rest in Me to manifest My knowing.

3. "Throughout long aeons he walks the path of dark to find the path of Light which leads to Me.

4. "For I say that refoldment into Self of Me is not known by man for long aeons, e'en as Self of Me is not known by him as Self of him for long, long aeons.

5. "In man's thinking, man begins to live as he leaves the mother-womb which borned him. And when he returns the clay of him to clay of earth, he thinks of life as ending, knowing not that its beginning never was, nor could its ending be.

6. "For I say that life is alone in Light of Me; as love and knowing are alone in Me.

7. "Tell thou to man that he who thinks life lives

23

in him, knowing not My life in him, dies as often as he lives to die again. But he who lives to manifest Me, knowing Me in him, never dies.

8. "When aeons pass and immortal man walks My path, full knowing his immortality, then shall he know My rest from whence cometh his power to manifest Me worthily.

9. "The Light of My all-knowing, power and presence shall then be man's in the measure of his knowing.

10. "Hark you, therefore, to My counselling. And write it down for man in words which are Mine and thine, not thine alone.

11. "For man's new day is dawning when the many who have alone known the anguish of the dark shall find rest through knowing the Light of Me in him as very Self of him."

V

1. "Write thou, therefore, that he who would find rest from burdens of his Earth must transcend his Earth and be not bound thereto. E'en far above the mountain tops of Earth he must rise into My kingdom of the Light which I AM, as he also is, when he knows he also is.

2. "Say to man these My very words.

3. "Behold in Me the fulcrum of My changing universe which but manifests change, though I change not, nor move.

4. "For I am Rest. In Me alone is Balance.

5. "He who would find power must know that he extends from Rest in Me, that I am he.

6. "He who would find Rest must return to Me, be Me; be fulcrum of his own power.

7. "For again I say, moving things have no power to move save through My will that they should move. And again I say, My will is but desire of My imaginings for manifesting My imaginings through form-imaged extensions of My thinking which manifest My knowing.

8. "Know thou, therefore, that power to move is in My will for things to move in obedience to desire in Me that moving things manifest My imagining.

9. "I center the moving shaft of My universe, yet I move not, though its power to move springs from Rest in Me.

10. "I center its growing systems, and changing cells of growing systems, yet I change not, e'en though their changing patterned waves spring from My eternal calm.

11. "I center seeming living things which reflect

*my power to manifest Me in them, but they live not;
I alone live.*

12. "My balanced thinking expresses life and energy which I alone AM, but the Thinker of the Cosmos is not the Cosmos, nor is the Cosmos the Thinker.

13. "Growing things are moving things in man's sensing, though they move not in man's knowing.

14. "Likewise moving things are changing things in man's sensing, though they change not in man's knowing.

15. "E'en though fast moving things of man's sensing move fast, they simulate My rest, while moving, from which they sprang into seeming motion.

16. "Again I say, My universe is but seeming forms of My imagining which seem to move to record the dual pulsing of My balanced thinking.

17. "Wherefore I say, the burdens of man are made by man in the image of his unbalanced thinking. Likewise the illnesses of man are fruit of his own making.

18. "Balanced thinking is an ecstasy which knows no burden, no fatigue nor imperfection.

19. "From man's own unbalanced thinking emanate the toxins of fatigue, and divers sicknesses, and fears.

26

20. *"Wherefore I say, come unto Me, ye self-burdened. Find rest in Me by being Me."*

These are the words of thy Creator, and mine, written truly from His illumining in me upon the mountain top.

"WHO AM I?"

"There is but one process of thinking for there is but One Mind. There are not two Minds nor two methods of thinking; nor are there two sets of laws governing thinking.

"Nor are there two separate substances, nor two separate things nor two separate beings in My universe.

"All thinking is universal thinking.

"All thinking things are thinking in unison.

"All are creating that which they are thinking.

"All thinking Beings are Self creating.

"All thinking Beings are creating all things.

"Man is Creator of himself.

"Man is the Creator of all that is.

"When man shall know My language of Light then shall he know My Voice.

"My still small Voice within universal man speaks to him in the language of Light, in words and tones, —and rhythmic waves extended from My Light."

"Within the heart of thinking man My Silent Voice has forever asked:

'WHO AM I?'

"WHO AM I?"

"Since the beginning man cried aloud, 'Who am I?'

"And My Voice forever answers, Thou Art I. I, the Universal One, am thou whom thou art creating in My image.

"I am I. I am I whom I am creating. I am the universal I.

"I am all that is, and Thee.

"I am He that is One with Me.

"I am the empire of I that am I."

"Since the beginning My Voice within man forever asks:

'WHENCE CAME I?'

"And My Voice forever answers:

"I came from God.

"I am of God.

"I am Soul, record of Idea.

"Where God is I am.

"Where I am there God is."

"Within man My eternal Voice demands:

'WHAT AM I?'

"And My familiar Voice within man answers:

"I am of the body of God, born of His substance.

"God is Mind. I am Mind.

"God is Truth. I am Truth.

"God is Love. I am Love.

"God is Life. I am Life.

"God is Light. I am Light.

"God is Power. I am Power.

"God is Rest and Balance. I am Rest and Balance.

"What God is, I am. What He commands, I command.

"My purpose is His purpose.

"God lives in me. My inheritance is from God and of God.

"He gives His all to me. He withholds nothing.

"The Divinity of me is Thine and mine. It is that which is recorded within the Soul of me. It is the Holy Spirit within the sanctuary of me.

"I am an Idea of Thine. The body of me is the Idea of the Soul of me. It is Thine and mine.

"I am the Master Sculptor. My body is the plastic clay. My Soul is the mother-mould of my body, the matrix for my regeneration.

"I am what I am.

"I shall be what I desire to be.

"What I am I have desired to be.

"I am the sum of my own desire.

"I am Thou, Creator of myself.

"Thou art I, Creator of all.

"I am Thou, Creator of All; for Thou has made it known in my heart that I am not of myself alone.

"WHO AM I?"

"*I am Thou and Thou art I.*

"*I am of the farthermost star and of the blade of grass in my door yard. I am of my brother and of the mountain.*

"*The ecstasy of my thinking varies the spectra of ten times ten billion stars and illumines the ether of endless space.*

"*Thy thinking has created all that is.*

"*My thinking is Thy thinking.*

"*My thinking has created all that is.*

"*I am ecstatic man.*

"*I am man, Self creating.*

"*I am God, Creator of man.*

"*I am Father of myself.*

"*I am Son of the living God.*

"*The ends of space are mine. I shall know no limitations that are not Thy limitations.*"

"*Within man My still small Voice asks ceaselessly:*

'WHY AM I?'

"*And my Voice answers:*

"*I am an expression of the universal passion of Creation.*

"*God created me that I should fulfill His purpose. God gave me desire to create and the power of Creation.*

31

"*God dwells within me. I shall not deny the power within me which is God within me.*

"*I shall not close the ears of my Soul to the whisperings of my Soul, which makes me dwell on the mountain top in ecstasy of inner thinking.*

"*The universal desire is expression of Idea through the rhythm of thinking, in accord with the law, in endless sequence throughout endless space.*"

"*Within man My ever questioning universal Voice beseeches:*

'WHITHER AM I BOUND?'

"*And My Voice answers:*

"*God was my beginning, is my substance and shall be my end.*

"*From the One I came. To the One I return.*

"*I but tarry by the way to do the will of the One.*

"*I am universal man, the image of my Creator. Ecstasy and exaltation attend me, for I know that all that is, is within me.*

"*My dwelling place is in the high heavens on the mountain top, above the waters and the earth.*

"*I range the high heavens in ecstasy.*

"*My feet are wings.*

"*The ends of space are mine.*

"*I sing praises unto all the universe by the way. The hosts of heaven rejoice with me by the way.*

"WHO AM I?"

"*I have denied my unity. My universality I have not known.*

"*My dwelling place was the earth. I walked the earth heavily in chains.*

"*My earth-bound feet dragged heavily after me. I wearied of the long road.*

"*My back bent with the ache of its burden.*

"*I was lonely and the way dark.*

"*I shall not deny my Oneness and live in the loneliness of the dark.*

"*I shall know my universality and I shall dwell on the mountain top in the Light of inner knowing.*

"*Hope dwells in the Light.*

"*Despair lurks in the dark.*

"*Life and growth are of the Light.*

"*Death and destruction are of the dark.*"

COSMIC MESSENGERS

When man gives to other men the inspiration which has come to him, he is a cosmic messenger of the living God delivering to man his revelation from the Holy of Holies.

The genius, the super-thinker with imagination who brings beauty to the world, is inspired man thinking in Light.

The greater the imagination, the greater the perception of the reality of universal existence; hence the greater the intelligence.

The lesser the imagination, the greater the illusion of existence.

The greater the imagination, the nearer to Oneness and the farther from separateness.

The inspired genius of great imagination has great knowledge.

He is able to use his knowledge creatively.

Those things which he desires to know, he may know.

The humble poet, inspired by knowledge conveyed to him by contemplation of the orbs of night, may give to man a message of truth which will outlive long generations of the learned whose disproved facts have died in the proving.

Genius is the forerunner of civilization.

Genius knows the ecstasy of the high heavens and the mountain top.

Genius is the bridge between man and God. He who wills may cross it.

Genius is locked within the Soul of every man. He who wills may unlock its doors and know its ecstasy.

Genius gives to man that which alone endures, which man has named "Art." No work of man can endure which is not born of inspiration and created in ecstasy.

Genius gives to man idea, rhythm and form, which are of the Soul and beyond which, in the created universe, there is nothing.

Genius knows no limitations within those which are universal.

Genius knows love and truth in all their fullness.

Genius translates the word of the universal One into the word of man for the Soul of man.

They who attain the ecstasy of genius are ordained messengers of the universal One.

Genius lifts man from the lowly stage of ferment. Man still is new. He is still but in the ferment.

Genius lifts brute man to gentle man.

Genius gives to man the harmonies of universal rhythm without which all is discord.

Genius gives to man knowledge which is of the Soul.

He who tunes his heart to the messages of genius purifies himself. No impurity can there be in his heart for verily he then is in communion with the Holy One.

The pure in heart know their universality.

Man may know his Oneness in the Light.

He who listens to the translations of genius knows the word of Creation. He knows the rhythms of the universal language of Light.

Genius awaits him who listens. The messages of genius are for the Soul of man. The senses of man comprehend them not.

To him whose Soul is quickened into ecstasy, God speaks from the trees of the forest and he understands.

To him the Silent Voice of Nature speaks, with understanding, from the babbling brook and the pounding sea. He knows all things.

To him universal Mind unfolds truth from the light of the sun and the blue dome of the heavens. He has all knowledge.

To him the rosy dawn and the golden autumn

36

sing messages which are to him as an anointing from the Holy One. He knows no limitations.

He who has not ears of the Soul to hear crucifies genius. The penalty of genius is crucifixion. The reward of genius is immortality.

Whom man crucifies does he glorify with immortality.

"Seven cities warr'd for Homer being dead
Who living had no roofe to shroud his head."

Genius desires no reward. The glory of genius is humility. Genius knows not the taint of arrogance.

The genius has all knowledge within himself. Inspiration will unlock the doors of all knowledge.

All knowledge exists in its entirety in all the universe.

All knowledge, being universal, exists in man.

The universe is omniscient, omnipotent and omnipresent.

SALUTATION TO THE DAY

The dawn telleth the coming of the new day.

I turn my eyes to the morning and purge myself in the purity of the dawn.

My Soul quickeneth with the beauty of the dawn.

Today is, and will be.

Yesterday was, and has been.

My yesterday is what I made it. I see it in memory, perfect or imperfect.

My today is what I will to make it. I will to make it perfect.

I am man. I have free right to choose. I may do as I will to do.

I have the power to build the day or to rend the day.

The day will be of my making, either perfect or imperfect, good or bad as I choose to live it in spirit or in flesh, on the mountain top or earthbound.

The day is of my choosing. None shall stay my hand in the making of the day.

If I rend the day I build ten other days, mayhap ten times ten, to undo the rending.

The Universal One will not allow this day to go unlived to the glory of Him whom I am nor to the fulfillment of His command, nor to the fulfillment of His purposes.

If I build the day I will have lived the day to the glory of the One in the fulfillment of that part of His purpose which is mine to fulfill.

So that I may meet the day with knowledge to build the day, I will look into my Soul while it is yet dawn, before the morning breaketh.

These are the words with which I greet the day.

These are words of the morning.

This is the spirit of the dawn.

This is the thought with which I meet the day which descendeth upon me and which cannot be turned away.

Who am I?

I alone am not I.

Thou, my Father, art I.

I am favored of Thee, my Creator.

I am of the Inner Mind.

I know the ecstasy and exaltation of genius.

All power is mine.

I know my omnipotence.

I have all knowledge.

I know my omniscience.

To me the universe is an open book.

I need not to learn. I know.

I see the unseen from the mountain top.

I hear the music of the spheres.

I know the transcendent joy of Creation.

I know my universality.

I am the Light of universal thinking.

I translate the language of light into the words of man for those who know not their universality.

Immortality is mine.

I will earn immortality.

I will bestow immortality.

Mine is the power to give immortality. I shall not deny that which shall give immortality to those who dwell in darkness and who reach out for the light.

I will reach out my hand into the darkness and lead him that asketh into the light.

I will keep my body charged with energy for the fulfillment of my purpose, in accord with that which is commanded of me.

I have knowledge of my body, through age long memory of the building of my body.

The power of the dynamic universe is behind my thinking.

I have the power of self-vitalization and re-vitalization of my body to multiply its productivity, in fulfillment of that which is commanded of me.

I have power to revitalize others whom I have made to believe. To him who believes I will give power to do that which is his to do for the glory of man and the glory of the One.

I stand on the electrodes of the universe of energy.

Power is mine to give by the wayside.

I will not deny to any man who asketh the power which is mine to give.

I have no limitations. Unlimited power is mine within those which are universal.

I will do today that which is of today and pay no heed to the tomorrow, nor waste regrets on that which was yesterday.

My day shall be filled to overflowing, yet shall I not haste the day; nor shall I waste the day.

Those things which I must do I shall desire to do.

A menial task which must be mine, that shall I glorify—and make an art of it.

Defeat I shall not know. It shall not touch me.

I will meet it with true thinking. Resisting it will be my strengthening.

But if, perchance, the day shall give to me the bitter cup, it shall sweeten in the drinking.

Courtesy will be in my heart to give to all.

My joy will be in serving.

My power will be in thinking true.

My power will be in knowing.

My power will be in humility. The taint of arrogance will I not know.

That which is I, will I keep within the shadow of the beautiful temple of modesty, but my doings will I send forth into the light that all may see; therefore, must my doings be true.

Force will I meet with gentleness; impatience with patience.

Truth will guide my footsteps through tortuous paths and lead me to the glory of the day's golden evening.

I will see beauty and goodness in all things. From all that is unlovely will my vision be immune.

God dwelleth in me. All that God hath to give He giveth me. He withholdeth nothing.

Blessed be the new day which descendeth upon me. I greet thee, O day. I cross Thy threshold with joy and thanksgiving.

My eyes are in the high heavens as I enter thy sacred temple.

I will sing the day through with a glad song, that the problems of the day shall be as chaff before the wind and that others may harken to my song and be quickened.

My countenance shall reflect the Spirit within me, that all may see.

Descend upon me O blessed day of opportunity. Thou shall not find me wanting.

INVOCATION FOR THE NIGHT

My day is done. The portals of Thy night encircle me. The Peace of Thy Rest encompasseth me.

To Thy heavens decentrate me, O my Father, and thus renew me for reconcentrating upon Mother Earth for one more day of manifesting Thee.

I feel Thee coming, ever coming, to sever Spirit of me from its sensed clay to take back to Source of me for reborning with its sensed clay image at the dawn.

Unto the calm of Thy Light, O Lord of day and night, take Light of me to rest in Thee for renewing when dawn reborns from night.

Destroy Thou that ego which is not Thee in me. Let my Self be Thy Self in me.

Let Soul of me be patterned by Thy rhythmic thinking.

Meld Thou Thy Light and mine.

Dissolve Thou my separateness and make me One with Thee.

Unite Thou me with Thee by voiding me.

Exalt Thou me. Take Thou me unto Thy high mountain top in ecstasy, that my morrow may reflect Thy glory in manifesting Thee.

Within the Oneness of Thy spirit let me find surcease from action, as waves of ocean find surcease in ocean's calm.

And in my surcease from body sensing, give to me Thy Omnipotential power to manifest Thy rest in balanced actions of my new day.

And in those actions of my morrow, intensify Thou my awareness of Light of Thee, centering Thy image in clayed form of me.

Give me to know those things I now know not, that I may be reborn with just one whit more of Light of Thy Omniscience centering my feeble knowing.

From Thy all-existent knowing, give to me Thy all-knowing, day by day, that I may more strongly manifest Thee in each morrow.

Upon my heart those unsolved problems of my day are plainly writ for solving in Thy Light for my new day.

O Thou Lord of the high heavens and earths of Thy imaged mortal Self, re-illumine Thou the pale Light of my veiled immortality while upon a shelf of Earth I lay my slowly pulsing mortal clay to die its nightly death for daily resurrection.

Re-attune the discords of my malpatterned thinking with the harmonies of Thy balanced rhythmic thinking.

44

Let the measure of Thy thinking be my measure, Thy rhythm be mine.

Resound the pulsing of my heartbeat to synchronize with Thine.

Immunize Thou my man-formed clay from toxins of unrhythmic pulsing begot from unbalanced thinking and from wrong action.

Void Thou the fears of my unknowing of the Light when my path is thereby made dark.

Thus fortify Thou my de-sensed clay, image of Thy imagining and mine, for greater mirroring of Thy Light through Light of me.

Thus balance Thou my imagining with Thine that my imagining may be wholly Thine.

Thus reinspire me with more knowing of Thy purpose that I may more worthily fulfill Thy purpose.

Thus cleanse the clay of me. Balance it in rhythms of Thy balanced thinking, to purify it in Truth for its new day of manifesting Thee.

Enfold Thou my Spirit, O heavenly night. Enshroud Thou me in Thy veiled mysteries, and deliver my resurrected clay to dawn, again renewed, again made whole.

Reborn Thou me in Thy Consciousness that I may again sing the glad song of one more cosmic day in Light of new knowing.

To Thee, O Father of Thy heaven of this Earth where Thou hast set me to serve Thee worthily, I commend my Spirit Soul in forgetfulness of all else but Light of Thee.

PART II

TEN LECTURES

ALL MOTION IS A SIMULTA-
NEOUS EXTENSION FROM AND
TO THE ONE STILL LIGHT

I

MAN'S PURPOSE ON EARTH

My text from THE DIVINE ILIAD consists of a very few words, but these few words are potent with much meaning:

"Seek Me. Know Me. Be Me. All men will come to Me in due time, but theirs is the agony of awaiting."

These few all-inclusive words clearly state the purpose of man on earth: *"Seek Me."* The purpose of man on earth is to seek God and find Him within himself.

"Know Me." The purpose of man on earth is to seek happiness and peace through knowledge of God. Man finds happiness only in the measure of his knowledge of God and obedience to His law.

"Be Me." The purpose of man on earth, therefore, is to *seek* God, *know* God and *be* God by finding the kingdom of heaven.

When man finds the kingdom of heaven he will *"know all things."* That is what Jesus meant when He said: *"Seek ye first the kingdom of God and His righteousness, and all these things shall be added unto you."*

The only way that man can fulfill his purpose of finding God is by way of a series of transforming experiences occupying millions of years. Each experience of man during these millions of years gradually transforms him by giving him new knowledge of the nature of God. New knowledge renews the mind.

Paul said, *"Therefore, be ye transformed by the renewing of your mind."* The only way that man can be transformed is by the renewing of his mind by knowing God's law. The word *righteousness* as used by Jesus meant balanced human relations under the law.

The transformation of man from the jungle to the mountain top is a mental one. It is a slow journey, from body sensing to mental Consciousness; from electrical awareness of body to cosmic awareness of the spiritual man manifesting God through the body.

Gradually this transformation of man has been taking place since his beginning. Time means nothing in the creative process. Man takes all the time he needs, but he who gains even one moment of time in the reconstruction or the transformation of himself advances that much nearer to the head of his class. Therefore, it is essential that we who wish to be transformed become aware of God in us so that we may know His secrets—that we may know His purpose—that we may know and understand the play of *cause* and *effect* which He has written for you and me to manifest.

Aeons of time pass during which we gradually come to know our purpose. Word by word and line by line we slowly become aware of our parts in the play, but the agony of awaiting that knowledge is ours. *"All men will come to Me in due time, but theirs is the agony of awaiting."* Seek ye first, last and always the kingdom of heaven, for there is nothing else we have done since we became an amoeba, polarized in the ooze of the planet by the light of the sun, until we have reached the top of our high mountain. That is all we ever do, forever and forever, during countless lives—we just keep on searching for the kingdom of heaven within us.

It is a long journey—a tremendous journey. It is the ageless journey of immortal man seeking recognition of his immortality through his mortality. When mortal man finally finds his immortality, he finds that for which he is searching, and knows it as God.

The two universes in which we live and have our being are the universe of sensing, from which we gain our information from impressions of happenings and experiences, and the mental universe from which we get our knowledge. Knowledge may come to us through our senses by transforming sensed impressions to our Consciousness through meditation, or it may come to us directly from the Cosmos by inspiration.

Information is but a record imprinted upon the brain of HOW to do things, of which we know not the WHY. Until we know the WHY, we have no knowledge. All down the centuries, right up to this day, man has had but little knowledge and much information. He has known HOW to produce marvelous effects but he does not know the cause of those effects.

We must know the *cause* of that which we have been cognizant of and satisfied with as *effect*. To be aware of effect is to be informed of the physical nature of the universe. Everyone can be informed of the physical nature of the universe and still lack knowledge. Until he begins to KNOW, he is still man in the body quite unaware of the kingdom of heaven within him. Until man begins to be inspired from the Cosmos and gain knowledge directly from the Source of all knowledge, he is still sensed man of the flesh and his genius has not unfolded.

Although we have reached a far stage in our search for God, we are still in our barbarian stage of unfoldment. We are still conquering, killing and exploiting our fellow men for self profit and, in con-

52

sequence, breeding fear and hate. But there *is* hope, for we are at the eve of a transition toward a so much greater knowledge of God. Our whole civilization will be lifted to a higher level if the seed of this *new* knowledge spreads fast enough to offset the seeds of *old* thinking and practices.

We are deceived by the seeming advancement of science into believing that we are highly civilized. As long as we have not arrived at a point in which we know the nature of God sufficiently to know of our unity with our fellow man, to make it unthinkable to even hurt another, much less kill, rob or exploit him, we are still uncivilized barbarians.

We are just reaching the point where we know that we hurt ourselves when we hurt another—that when we break God's law, His law breaks us to an equal extent—that the Sermon on the Mount and the Golden Rule are not just good advice given abstractly to accept or reject as we choose, but that inviolate cosmic law lies behind them. We are just becoming aware that we must readjust all our human relations to conform to God's law or perish periodically by utter degradation of our hard built civilizations.

We are actually at a point of threatened destruction of our present civilization because of having made our own law of might against right, and having practiced it in the building of our empires by

53

forcibly taking from our fellow men that which we wanted for ourselves, and enslaving them under our lordship.

We have learned that *"He who lives by the sword shall die by the sword"* is cosmic law and not just an abstraction. The whole world has paid dearly for that lesson by reaping the frightful harvest of the seeds of hate, fear and greed it has sown. For every man the world has killed, it has paid tenfold in blood. Its treasuries, filled with our robbing, have been emptied by robbers whom we have ourselves created to rob and kill us. Our present civilization is dying as a result of its self-inflicted ills.

We must learn that this electric universe of motion is divided into wave cycles which are equally divided into opposite expressions. Also that our actions in all of our human relations are wave cycles which must balance their actions of giving with their consequent reactions of regiving. Likewise we must learn that the giving half of each cycle must precede the regiving. When we learn to practice that inexorable law of Nature fully, civilization will then progress steadily and mankind will find happiness in its resultant unity. Until that time comes in man's unfolding, he will continually be broken to the extent of his own breaking of cosmic law.

Our only hope of a resurrection of our dying civilization lies in a sufficiently greater comprehension of the nature of the God for whom mankind is searching to enable him to both comprehend and obey God's cosmic law of love upon which His universe is founded.

When we learn that Nature never takes anything which is not given, and that the cosmic law of love is based upon giving and regiving equally, we shall have advanced far toward our spiritual goal. Likewise, when we practice that law of *rhythmic balanced interchange* in all transactions between the opposites of Nature, we shall have advanced so far physically that our entire civilization will be assured of its eternal continuity instead of being continually condemned to periodic destruction.

Man's purpose on earth is to build happiness, peace and good will on earth. He can find peace, happiness and good will only as he ceases building chaos. He has been building chaos and expecting his chaos to crystallize into a unity. That is impossible. It is incredible that man cannot see the impossibility of finding peace and happiness through practices which make peace and happiness impossible.

The time has now come when man must find that the whole universe is purposeful, and that each thing must fulfill its purpose. Also he must find that purposefulness lies in the direction of law and order, not in the direction of chaos.

It has taken man a long time to arrive even at this

state of unfoldment where he now knows that greed, selfishness and disunity cannot build a stable civilization. The incredible thing is that he thought it could.

Millions of years ago, he began his journey as an actor in this divine drama unaware of a single line of his part, learning it line by line, experience by experience—down through the ages from one incarnation to another—from body to body—from record of Soul and body to record of Soul and body—a continuity of life which began in the beginning for every one as an individual single cell. An individuality has kept pace with its gradual growth as each actor fulfilled his purpose on earth by playing his part line by line as it came to him out of the dark.

Once when I was in Washington, some people told me there was a very interesting machine that counts, adds, subtracts, multiplies and calculates the most complex mathematical problems, accomplishing in a few moments what a great mathematician could not finish in months. It took years to make this machine for there were many thousands of parts to it and experimentation was in process for years.

I was invited to see that machine. When I got there, a few little parts of it were assembled. They were working, doing something collectively, but the greater part of it was distributed and in boxes. There were thousands of separate little pieces of metal,—

large pieces—wheels with gears—shining metals and dull metals—castings and finely cut parts—big and little—complex and simple—lying all around the great room on chairs and in boxes—all numbered as to their place and purpose.

Now imagine some of the parts of that machine saying, "Well, what are we here for? What is this all about? What is the purpose of all this? They take us out and bore holes in us and put us back again—they bore another hole and put us together in groups and try to make us work at something—then they put us back again. They change our shape and recast us in another metal—then they polish us. It has all been going on for so long and not one of us knows what it is all about. It all seems foolish." And another big wheel might say, "I am beginning to see the purpose of this. They have tried me out and at last I am beginning to see what it is all about. I seem to feel that we are all just extensions of each other, all made to manifest some one purpose."

Some geniuses or mystics are now at that stage in our civilization where they know that all men are extensions of each other. Some go farther and actually KNOW what it is all about.

Eventually they put that machine all together, and got it working. Each part was then aware that it was an essential part of the whole. Each knew that not one of those parts could be left out without impairing the whole. They knew that each of those many parts was a unit. For the first time they began to see their purposefulness, and realized the necessity of expressing individual perfection in the fulfillment of their collective purpose. They then knew that all were *one*.

Man must begin to see the unitary principle of man—knowing that there are not separate men or separate individuals, but that the whole man idea is one. He must know that all mankind is connected with every other part of mankind, all geared together by the one omnipresent Light of God which centers all as ONE and motivates all as ONE. Until man knows that separation from God is impossible, even for one second, he does not begin to have knowledge.

In our search for God, there are so many things we do have to know in order to comprehend His law, and we cannot obey it until we do comprehend it. In one hundred years there has been a vast physical transformation of all civilization through greater advancement given to us by the great scientific geniuses who have learned HOW to do things with matter and the forces of Nature. But when you ask science the WHY of things, science flounders. Scientists say, "All we know is that the universe is light, just electric waves of light. We have only recently acquired that information. Only within the last twenty-five years have we become aware that the whole universe of matter, your body and mine, trees, suns and planets, are just waves of light." Science has also said, "If we knew the secret of Light we would have a new civilization—we might even become aware of God through knowing that secret."

There is the answer to that new civilization that is coming now, for we are going to know the secret of Light and we are going to be aware of the nature of God. Man has never been aware of the nature of God; in fact, it has often been declared that the human mind could never comprehend God. That statement has been based upon the assumption that the reason we could never comprehend God is that our *senses could not detect* God.

It is true that we cannot see God but we can KNOW Him. And therein is the essence of New Age thinking. The next hundred years will see as great a spiritual advance in the culture of our civilization as it has seen physically during the past hundred years. That which we cannot see, we can KNOW. We can see the bodies of men but we cannot see man, for the supreme Being within man is invisible. He cannot be seen. He can only be known. For the same reason we cannot see God but we can know Him, and we can know the nature of God by knowing His laws and creative processes.

When we know the nature of God sufficiently to reflect His nature in us, we become God to the extent of our ability to reflect His nature in us. By knowing the secret of Light, we will know the mystery of life and death—of reincarnation, of matter and space, and the relationship of suns to planets.

The more we know the Light, the more we shall realize our purpose in manifesting that Light gloriously. Every moment of life in the Light is a moment of glorification in the awareness of our omnipotence in manifesting the Light.

Someone once asked Toscanini's son: "What was the highest point in your father's life?" The answer was: "Every point in it is his highest point. He lives gloriously and fully every moment of his life, whether conducting an orchestra or peeling an orange."

That is what we must do when we fully know the purposefulness of life—live it gloriously by living it ecstatically. We can live it ecstatically only as we know the ecstatic nature of God and become like Him through being continually inspired by communion with Him. To become like Him, we must become aware of our identity with Him. We must know Him as Creator of all that is, and in so doing know ourselves as creator of all that is.

God's one purpose is to express His will by giving of His love in the fulfillment of His law. Our one purpose is to give love in conformity with the law. God has no other purpose, nor has man. Nature expresses that purpose in every action which records God's knowing through His thinking.

The more we find the God of our searching, the more we know Him and become like Him. That is what I mean by the perpetual transformation of man, as man more fully knows his purpose on earth by continually finding the kingdom of heaven within him. That is also what I mean by constant communion with God, communion of identity which is Oneness, not communion with Him as though He were another.

The more we thus know God, the less we pray in the traditional customary sense, which means finding words to express our desire periodically whenever we feel that there is something to ask for. Whenever I feel that ecstasy of love in me, I know that God and I are working together as ONE, not He and me, but just ONE. When I am inspired to create with Him as ONE, I know that His knowing and His thinking are my knowing and my thinking. My works are always masterly when I am thus ONE with the Light, for I know that I am giving out God's love as commanded of me. I know that my inspiration is God's Silent Voice being recorded through me.

That ecstatic love state of my Consciousness is my forever prayer which gives me my desires because of knowing God's desires. Whenever I am in that state, I am praying, and whenever the demands of earth and body cut me off from that continuous state of communion, then things go wrong. Work done then is not masterly. All the little troubles of earth and ills of body pile up in front of me to become mountains until I am again in the Light of love. When that happens, all inharmonies disappear—needed supply comes toward me instead of my seeking it— ills of body are as though they were not—and omnipotential power is mine again.

Thus it is that humanity flounders purposelessly because of being unaware of purpose. Thus it is that weaknesses, fears and illnesses attack the bodies of individual and collective man whenever he fails to manifest God's will by the giving of love.

Normalcy of body and mind can come only to him who is a purposeful part of Nature. So long as purposefulness is manifested by any unit of God's Creation, just so long will normalcy of that unit continue. The slightest breach of the law is instantly balanced by recording abnormalcy in that unit. The measure of such recorded abnormalcy is the measure of that breach of the law.

In this manner the units of Nature which are expressing their purposefulness are continued in normalcy throughout their cycles, while those which breach their normalcy are attended with the consequences of their unbalanced actions.

Nature thus manifests its law by getting rid of purposeless units, for as soon as any of them cease to be purposeful by expressing the universal love principle, Nature shortens their cycles to eliminate them.

Anger, for example, is not love; therefore it is not a purposeful manifestation of the fundamental principle of Nature. He who expresses anger breaks the universal law of love. For so doing, that law breaks him by creating toxic effects within his body in the measure of his own self-condemnation.

This is a balanced universe of love. Every wave of God's thinking records that absolute balance of love. Every unbalanced wave of man's thinking creates distortions which must be balanced by himself. These distortions do not affect the balance of the universe. Its purposefulness continues in its balanced expression of universal law.

Consider our present civilization in this light. Is it not plainly evident that mankind has been break-

ing the law so violently that he has himself condemned himself to self-destruction? The whole
world body is sick unto death for its flagrant breach
of purposefulness by breeding hate and fear through
manifesting greed instead of manifesting the love
nature of God.

The entirety of civilization is slated for self-
destruction for that reason, and its only chance for
a renaissance lies in replacing greed with love in all
human relations. Over and over again man has
broken himself by thus disobeying the law, and he
will forever continue to break himself until he comprehends the law sufficiently to obey it.

Through comprehension man can save himself.
That is what Paul meant when he said: *"Therefore,
be ye transformed by the renewing of your mind."*
When we know the fulcrum-and-lever principle of
the wave, we shall know the Father-Mother principle of this creating universe.

We shall comprehend the mechanics of that principle as applied to every action in Nature. We shall
then comprehend that the universe is merely an electric record of God's thinking. The whole product of
His thinking is in formed body images of His knowing. That is what the universe is, the ONE IDEA
of God's knowing divided into the many ideas of His

thinking, and those many ideas multiplied into count-less units of formed bodies of those many ideas.

The forms thus recorded never become the ideas. That which is God never becomes matter. That which is the still Light is extended into the two moving lights to record God's knowing by His thinking, but we who are the imaged record of that thinking are not the idea from which we are extended. Our bodies are but the extensions of our God-Selves.

Creator and Creation might thus be reduced to the following simple formulæ expressed in several word-groups but all of the same meaning.

KNOWING—THINKING—PRODUCT

OR

POWER—EXPRESSION OF POWER—RESULT

OR

STILLNESS—ACTION—RECORD OF ACTION

OR

LIGHT—LIGHT-WAVES—MATTER

OR

FULCRUM—WAVE LEVER—MOTION

OR

MAGNETIC LIGHT—ELECTRICITY—REFLECTION

OR

REALITY—IMAGINATION—UNREAL IMAGE

OR

SEXLESSNESS——FATHER-MOTHER——FORMED BODIES

OR

IDEA——DIVISION OF IDEA——PROJECTION

OR

ONENESS——POSITIVE-NEGATIVE——ILLUSION

OR

LOVE——GIVING-REGIVING——REPETITION

OR

LIFE——LIFE-DEATH——REBIRTH

OR

CAUSE——EXPRESSION——EFFECT

OR

GOD——DESIRE IN GOD——THE UNIVERSE

And so up to this time we have been floundering around in these questions of life and death, emotions, love, hate, greed and selfishness. We have been accumulating things, material things to possess, things of earth which must be returned to earth. Our ideas of wealth and power have been based upon what our bodies needed. For that reason we became selfish, greedy, cruel and brutal. Humans became inhuman—beastly—by killing, robbing and enslaving other humans.

The more religiously devout we became, the more inhuman we became—even to the point of devoutly asking God to aid us in our inhumanity by helping us to kill. Also, up to this time our search for the

66

One God has bred many religions based upon false concepts of God. God is our Father. We are His beloved children, Light extensions of His very Self. God is love, yet practically all religions conceive Him as an angry, wrathful god, ever ready to inflict terrible punishment upon his sinful, wicked children, a god of sorrows, capable of suffering deep anguish because of our transgressions.

Instead of searching for a God of Light within ourselves, we have searched outside of ourselves for a god of form. We have demanded an extraneous god which our senses could visualize. For that reason we have made thousands upon thousands of gods of some imaged form carved in wood or stone, and worshipped those forms as idols.

Messengers of God, such as Jesus, have appeared at times to tell us the true nature of God. We invariably crucified them, then worshipped them after realizing their divinity.

Religion of today is largely idolatrous for the reason that our primacy demands a god who appeals to the senses. For that reason millions of men worship God *through* Buddha, Jesus, Mohammed and other messengers, whose form they can sense as visualized images of God.

Those who do so have not yet unfolded sufficiently to *know* God Himself as the I AM of all the universe. Those many millions would consider one to be a blasphemer who claimed that he walks and talks directly with God in close communion.

Yet mankind has unfolded to that state of Consciousness where there are many who have found the kingdom of heaven within themselves to such an extent that they no longer ask intercession from men of earth for the privilege of contacting God through them.

The mass of mankind still holds tight to the traditions of pagan and heathen superstitions and beliefs. These believe that ordained priests and ministers can save their Souls from sin through baptismal rites and ceremonies. They believe this to such an extent that if a child dies without being baptized, it will have no Soul, or that it will be cast into everlasting fires for having been born in sin. Such horrible beliefs indicate that barbaric state of the mass of today's humanity.

"Hell is paved with the skulls of innocent babes" is a common expression which evidences this horrible belief of many religions of today which still keep alive the blood beliefs and practices of pagan ancestors. The enlightened ones who have come to know God in them are fully aware that no human has any power whatsoever to remit the sins of another, or to

68

save or condemn his Soul, or to intercede for him with God. Man cannot ordain man with power to do anything which a man cannot do for himself by direct unity with God, for God centers every man, awaiting his awareness of that fact.

The coming age of new thinking will see the end of heathen and pagan religious practices for countless thousands—and these will become the seed for the ending of such practices in those of lesser knowing.

Thus man's search for God, which is his sole purpose on earth, will find great fulfillment in these coming days of man's new unfolding. The time has come for all mankind to know that there is nothing which stands between him and God, and that no man who has lived within a mere few thousand years out of all eternity should be worshipped in place of, or even as a symbol of, the eternal God of all Creation who created these men as He created you and me.

All God-worship through man is as idolatrous as the worship of God through graven images is idolatrous. When man *knows* God, he will no longer need to *sense* Him through formed images.

The time has now come when men must again be transformed into higher beings through new comprehension. In the cycle in which Jesus lived, he could not even tell His people those things He would tell them today. He then said: *"I have yet many things to say unto you, but ye cannot bear them now."* Now we are ready for new knowledge.

We are ready for our new day. In the last one hundred years we have been made ready for it. Our comprehension is greater. We know that what happens anywhere happens everywhere. Even one century ago man did not know that. We have been prepared to know things that man of one hundred years ago could not even begin to understand. God has raised our comprehension so that we shall understand Him when He talks directly to us through the Silent Voice of inspiration.

God has prepared us through His messengers—the mystics, geniuses, poets and musicians who have given us our culture. He has talked with us through His rhythms of the heavens by making them a part of us to quicken us with their ecstasy in our search for the kingdom of heaven. In this age of transition between *sensing* and *knowing,* we must acquire cosmic knowledge through the eyes and ears of the Spirit instead of those of the body. We must *know* how to find God by getting away from the body. We must know how to *talk* with God so that we *know* the nature of God. Moreover, we must *know* and *obey* God's law.

Many people say, " 'The Secret of Light' is quite

over my head. I get a little bit at a time." Thank God
if you even get a little at a time. The reason you get
a little at a time instead of much is simply because
the transition from sensing to knowing is a difficult
one. If you have been accustomed to acquiring information through the senses, that habit is so strong that
you just try to memorize what your senses have recorded on your brain instead of closing your book
and talking it over with God directly. That is the
only way you can KNOW anything. Your failure to
understand is because the sensed records you have
engraved upon your brain have no understanding in
them. Knowledge is cosmic. When you take your
sensed impressions into the Light of your Self and
ask that knowledge be revealed to you through the
Light, you will then have knowledge concerning
what you have been reading—and not until.

How often you have heard the expression "Be still
and know." To be still for the purpose of knowing
is to think your information back into the Light of
your inner Self until you have stopped thinking. Silent meditation fixes that *information* into your Consciousness as *knowledge*. Very few people do that.
They are quite content with storing vast quantities
of information upon their brains. Very few know
that they can talk it over with God by thinking it back
into His still Light which they also are. Those who

do know that acquire great knowledge and power to co-create with God.

Thinking is not easy. If you study music for the first time, you will find that out. You will be lucky if in half an hour your brain is not too tired to remember any more. You have only learned a few notes and made a few sounds which are not music. It takes months and months of doing that before you know music well enough to produce music instead of sound. Until that which you read from the notes reaches your very Soul, you do not *know* music nor can you *produce* music.

For this reason, everyone should bend every effort to make the transition from sensing to knowing so that his creations can be powerful and masterly interpretations of the Light of ALL-KNOWING instead of being parrot-like repetitions of memories stored in one's brain as information is stored in an encyclopedia.

It is only through thus adding to our knowledge that we become transformed to a greater awareness of our immortality. Like the little parts of the complex machine that serve their purpose only when they become one whole, so do we know our purpose on this journey only when we are enabled to forget our separateness by knowing the whole.

A man with a certain name lives at a certain address and thinks of himself as separate and apart from all Creation. A brook comes from the sea by way of the heavens. It seems to be a unit which is separated from everything else, but it is forever connected with the heavens and the sea. We do not see the connection between the heavens and the brook but they are, nevertheless, forever connected. Though we cannot *see* the connection, we can *know it*.

Likewise man cannot *see* his connection with his Source in the universal sea of Light, but he can *know* it. That is the very essence of the transition man is now undergoing which will transform him into a higher being.

The transformation will come through man's greater awareness of the Light within him. The more man becomes transformed through knowledge of the Light, the more he knows that his purpose in life is to find God in order to become one with Him.

II

THE LAW OF BALANCE

THE LAW OF BALANCE is the Law of Love upon which the universe is founded. This law is given to man for his coming renaissance of greater comprehension. It is, of all laws, the most inclusive and the most simple. It consists of but three words. These three words are the very foundation of all our material existence, all phenomena of matter or interchange between humans, economically, socially and spiritually.

I will read to you from *THE DIVINE ILIAD:*

"Great art is simple. My universe is great art, for it is simple.

"Great art is balanced. My universe is consummate art, for it is balanced simplicity.

"My universe is one in which many things have majestic measure; and again another many have measure too fine for sensing.

"Yet I have not one law for majestic things, and another law for things which are beyond the sensing.

"I have but one law for all My opposed pairs of creating things; and that law needs but one word to

spell it out, so hear Me when I say that the one word of My one law is

BALANCE.

"*And if man needs two words to aid him in his knowing of the workings of that law, those words are*

BALANCED INTERCHANGE.

"*If man still needs more words to aid his knowing of My one law, give to him another one, and let those three words be*

RHYTHMIC BALANCED
INTERCHANGE."

Balance is the foundation of all human relations —of the universe itself. The stars of heaven move in obedience to it. They cannot do otherwise. Cosmic disaster of untold dimension would follow such disobedience. The starry universe is so absolute in its balance that the movement of a dewdrop on any one planet necessitates the readjustment of the orbits of all the stars of heaven to that microcosmic event. Because of that law all happenings are universal. Any action anywhere is extended for repetition everywhere. All motion is as omnipresent as the Light of God is omnipresent. All effect is universal.

God is balance. From the stillness of His balance in the unconditioned One Light, He extends His balance to the conditioned universe of motion as two opposite unbalanced conditions of two lights which seek balance through each other.

Oppositely-conditioned pairs in Nature seek balance through each other by repeatedly giving all that each has to give to the other in rhythmic sequences. In Nature this process continues perpetually because in Nature all givings of one are perpetually balanced by equal regivings of the other. Nature never takes that which is not given.

This universe is founded upon love as manifested in the giving of one opposite to the other for regiving. The earth gives its forests to the heavens and the heavens give them back again to earth for equal regiving. Every dewdrop given by the heavens is equally regiven to the heavens by the earth.

Equal interchange between opposite conditions manifests the love principle of balance upon which God's universal body is founded. Whatever is true of God's universal body is true of man's body. It is the equality of balance between the giving and regiving of Nature which makes its transactions perpetual. The lack of the love principle of rhythmic balanced interchange in the transactions of men is the reason for the ills of the body and for the disasters which make continuance of relations between men impossible.

The seller of goods is also a buyer. If the seller gives less to his customers than the value of what he charges, he deprives his customer of the ability to regive that which the seller needs to again become a seller. By sacrificing the good-will which is the foundation of continuance in any business, the love principle has been subtracted from the transaction in the measure of inequality of interchange.

Neither man nor nation can continue an interchange of relations upon a harmonious basis of multiplying power when the universal love principle is violated. The law of balance is absolute. He who breaks that law will be equally broken by it.

If each of the two conditions which forms the basis for every transaction between pairs of opposites in Nature can be kept in balance with the other, the resultant effect is *good*. When they are out of balance with each other, the resultant effect is *bad*.

Good and bad—sin and evil—measure the degree in which all pairs of oppositely-conditioned effects of motion are either in balance with each other or out of it. In all our human relations we, ourselves, make our own good and bad, or evils and sins, by our desires and decisions to act either in or out of balance with Universal Law.

There is no sin or evil in Nature, for Nature observes the law of balance. Every unbalanced effect in Nature is balanced by its opposite unbalanced effect.

The play of Creation consists of dividing all idea into two opposite parts. What each half does in relation to the other half constitutes the play. Such divisions into halves are male and female—buyer and seller—positive and negative—compression and expansion, and countless other divisions of ideas into unbalanced pairs for the purpose of expressing those ideas.

Whatever these opposed pairs do in any transaction results in an effect. All human relations are thus divided, and transactions between humans result in either good or bad effects which we call happiness or misery in accordance with whether the transaction is balanced or unbalanced. Man can make whichever he chooses. He can make happiness, success, wealth, friendships and health only by obeying the law. He can never find them by disobeying the law.

For aeons mankind has been breaking the law in an endeavor to find happiness, wealth and power. Civilization has been built by the unbalanced power of might-over-right. Nations have enriched themselves by impoverishing other nations, expecting to find happiness by giving misery—expecting to attain power by depriving others of power. Without any exception, those who have broken the law have been equally broken by the law. This war-broken world

78

of today is the result of yesterday's breaking of the law.

Good, bad, evil, success or failure are not qualities of Nature. They are the product of man's actions resulting from his thinking; just as the product of his factories is the result of his thinking.

Man can manufacture a pair of shoes which cause him physical agony. If they do not fit his feet, they are out of balance with their purpose. He can also manufacture physical and mental agony by unbalanced actions and decisions regarding his domestic, business or social relations. All of man's troubles and blessings are manufactured by man.

Man manufactured the misery and agony which drenched the world with the blood of all nations by manufacturing the conditions which made that misery inevitable. In Nature all effects of motion repeat their kind as though mirrored from cause to effect. *Misery inflicted by greed and selfishness is radarred back to the giver as misery. Likewise the giver of love begets love by the same law.*

The law of love is absolute in Nature. It has no relation to morality, religion, sin, good or evil. It is the cause of all effect. The effect has no reality. Cause alone is.

One cannot sin against God. God's universe of love is balanced. Man cannot upset God's balance. He can but upset his own. He can create agony for himself or his fellow man by sinning against himself or his fellow man, but he cannot create agony for the God of love. God's Mind is eternally ecstatic. His Light is forever in equilibrium—at rest. God's Creation is perfect. To the God Mind all stages of the workings of Creation are always perfect. No matter how unbalanced or unrhythmic is the interchange between any of the opposites of creating things, that unbalance in them is balanced in God, just as the unbalance of the lever is balanced in its fulcrum.

In this respect I again quote from *THE DIVINE ILIAD: "All men will come to Me in due time, but theirs is the agony of awaiting."* That means the agony is man's alone, for man is manifesting God's idea of cause and effect in his Creation by unbalanced actions as well as by balanced ones.

For that reason man's prayers to God should be to ask for knowledge and wisdom to manifest God worthily in order that his thinking and his acting shall have the balance of the Light in them.

When we ask forgiveness for our trespasses as we forgive those who have trespassed against us, it should not be in the sense that we have trespassed against God, or caused Him grief or sorrow because of our acts, for that is impossible. It should be in the sense that we have trespassed against ourselves and our neighbors by breaking the law of rhythmic balanced interchange in our dealings with them. We thus hurt ourselves and every other man on earth by lowering the standard of all mankind. Conversely, every balanced act raises the standard of all mankind, but no unbalanced act can affect universal balance.

From the Creator's point of view, it is cause and effect working perfectly in accordance with Universal Law. Many of man's prayers ask God to violate Universal Law in order that man may escape the hurt brought on by his own unbalanced acts. All through the war, such prayers arose from every home and pulpit asking the balance of peace and love to arise from conditions of unbalance made by man himself. Many even blame God for their own actions. How often we have heard people say, "If there is a God of love, why does He permit such suffering in the world?" Many go farther and say that God is punishing man for his sins. Many talk of a god of wrath and a jealous god.

Such misconceptions of God and Creation arise from a complete misunderstanding of the quality of love which the Creator has for His Creation. This misunderstanding must be clarified. Man must know the attitude of God toward His Creation; also he must know Creation's processes.

Creation is the *imagined* effect of a *real* cause. The

cause is the desire of God to express His balanced, formless, changeless idea by dividing His idea into many parts, giving it many imagined forms, and setting those forms in motion to express the idea in sequences of changing events. *Motion and effect only seem. They have no reality.*

God's attitude toward His Creation of a universe of cause and effect is like a man's attitude toward his own creations. The playwright conceives an idea for a play. It must be based upon cause and effect, governed by the Universal Law of Love, for there is nothing in Creation which is not so based. He divides his concept into its many parts, unfolding a story that always depicts transactions between pairs of opposite conditions which manifest the working of Universal Law. He loves his concept, his imaginings, and all of the effects he is creating because of the balanced and unbalanced inter-relations between his characters working out the Law.

In the plot are good and bad, hero and villian, saint and sinner, dark and light, humor and pathos, happiness and agony, kindliness and intolerance. Without these there would be no play. The playwright loves each part of his creation equally with the whole as One Idea. To be a master playwright, each part must be true to Universal Law. Perfection for him means making everything work truthfully in balance with Universal Law.

During his entire period of creative expression, his mental attitude is that of ecstasy which always accompanies every masterful creation. There is no change of emotion in that ecstasy. He does not hate the villian, despise the meanness of the cheat in his play, or become angry because of intolerance of another character. Nor does he express the opposite emotions of joy, love or happiness because of those happenings which we call good in the play.

The Master Playwright could not do this if he would, for it is not in the nature of the unchanging God-Mind to express all of those different emotions at one time. These different emotions are but the imagining of different parts of the whole—and all imagined *parts* void each other in the whole. God's whole mental attitude is the changeless one of love for the whole, and ecstasy for the fulfillment of His desire to create.

God, the Master Playwright, is Master Creator. The Universal Play of Creation is His imagining. His mental attitude is one unchanging ecstasy in knowing that the unfoldings of His imaginings are true to His law.

Even the most minute of microcosmic events

which manifests His imaginings unfolds with as strict an observance to Universal Law as the most majestic event in His heavens.

As and when they unfold in accordance with Universal Law, His ecstasy for the fulfillment of His desire for creating the imaged forms of His imagining is unchanging. There are no emotions of grief, sorrow, anger, jealousy, or pity in the God-Mind because of the happenings to any pairs of His creating things. To Him it is all GOOD, for all of it is the working of Law.

Imagine how untrue to the nature of the unchanging God-Mind to feel the changing emotions of grief, anger, jealousy and other emotions at the same time, in relation to the countless happenings to the infinity of parts in the Master Playwright's play of Creation as manifested in His vast universe. To the Creator all is perfection.

That which man calls sin and evil are but experiences wherein two unbalanced conditions fail to demonstrate the law of balance by interchanging their two opposed conditions equally. That is all there is to any action whatsoever in God's creating universe.

If a machine created by man breaks down because of unbalanced interchange between its opposing parts, or because of overwork or lack of oil to lubricate its parts, we do not think of it as evil or sin com-

84

mitted by the machine, or by its creator or operator. We think of it as breaking the laws which govern the successful operation of the machine, as an accident or an experience. Such a breakdown of the machine may be due to bad judgment, negligence, ignorance or other causes, but in every case the cause of it is unbalanced interchange between its opposed interchanging parts and conditions—all traceable to cause and effect.

If man learns something from such a breakdown which will keep him from repeating the cause which led to the accident, he has profited thereby. If he fails to profit by the experience, he will have to again suffer the consequences of it until he does learn to profit by the lesson. In neither case has the thought of sin or evil been connected with the experience.

The same principle applies to man's human relations. When these are so extraordinarily out of balance that misery, agony or death is the resultant effect, man, individually or collectively, gradually learns a lesson which eventually keeps him from repeating the same breaches of the law. In the meantime, man suffers the effects of his breaches of the law, individually and collectively, by broken friendships, loss of health, failures in business, unhappiness in home, enmities, and countless other ill effects arising from his own creations. These culminate in such colossal disasters as world wars with their consequent wholesale carnage.

To relate any of the ills to sins against God is like relating a tornado to a sin against God. The tornado is the effect of unbalance between the two opposite temperature conditions. One condition is attempting to gain supremacy over the other by outbalancing the other. Universal Law will not permit this breach of the law between opposite weather conditions. The resultant damage is the ill effect of this breach just as damage to children's shins is the resultant effect of unbalance between opposite conditions when two children playing seesaw break the law of rhythmic balanced interchange while manifesting the law of balance in playing that game—or between two men who try to get the better of each other in a business transaction.

Likewise God is not angry with Earth because it generates an angry tornado nor is He grievous or sorrowful because of the damage which Earth perpetrates upon itself. Nor does He threaten the earth with punishment because of such *an unbalanced action.*

Earth punishes itself for that action by the hurt of it upon itself. The measure of the hurt is the measure of Earth's breach of the law.

The tornado is a perfect manifestation of the in-

86

evitable working of God's law. It is, therefore, *good* even to the hurt of it.

All of man's evil and sinful actions are, likewise, good—even though he is hurt by them. So-called sins and evil relate only to man. To God or Nature, they do not exist. To God, they are but perfect effect of cause. There is naught but good in the Light of Love from which the universe is begotten, for Love cannot beget anything but Love.

The secret of harmonious human relations lies in a deeper understanding of rhythmic balanced interchange between opposite unbalanced halves of all transactions. Unbalance is necessary in order for interchange to take place, for without two unbalanced conditions motion could not take place at all.

No matter how great the desire is to walk, one cannot do so until he loses his balance by dividing it into opposite halves to become the basis of a two-way moving cycle. With one unbalanced half, he takes one step, and recovers his balance with the other half of the cycle in order to take the next step. If the interchange is equal, he will walk steadily. If not, he will stagger or fall. He has not committed a sin against God or the universe by thus falling. He has merely hurt his own body and gained an experience in so doing.

Vapors rising from the ocean are balanced by rains

87

falling into it. The balance of this planet in its orbit is so perfect that an astronomer can tell to the split second where it is at any time—or when an eclipse of the sun or moon will take place.

If the earth should vary ever so slightly in its orbit and become out of balance with the other planets in this solar system, its oceans would rise over its highest mountains and sweep all expressions of life from its surface.

The perpetuity of Creation is based upon the constant giving of one half of a cycle to the other half for the purpose of repeating the creative process through another cycle of giving for regiving.

Living things breathe fully outward in order that they may breathe fully inward. Credits at the bank equal their debits. Repayment of credit simultaneously voids an equal debit. Compression in an engine is balanced always by an equal expansion. When an object which has been hurled into the air falls back to earth, it passes every point on its downward journey at the same speed of its upward journey.

Human happiness can come only by obeying Nature's law of giving in order that the other half of any transaction may equally regive. The greater one's comprehension of the Universal Law of Love, the greater is one's ability to obey it.

There are many mothers who bring grief to themselves and great unhappiness to their children by their sacrificial martyrdom. In truth they are not *giving*—they are *taking*.

In the business world, unwise men take more than they give. They do not realize that they are breaking the Universal Law which will eventually break them to an equal extent. It may not be balanced in the form of dollars and cents but in the loss of good-will upon which their future business depends.

Man's ignorance of the Law of Love in personal and world relationships will not serve as an excuse to save him from disaster.

Wealth cannot be acquired from others by might, for wealth thus taken will impoverish him who takes anything which is not given. Nor can power be thus acquired, for the weakness of the despoiled will prevail against the might of the despoiler.

Everywhere in the world this law is seen working out its inexorable certainty. Empires built by might are dissolving. Rich world treasuries are disgorging their gold and piling up debt. The blood of every man killed by the sword has been paid for by ten—perchance ten times ten—of those who killed. Nations which have fattened on the food taken from others are starving amid the ruins of palaces in which they feasted.

A new world—one world—cannot grow out of a

universe built on the foundations of hate and fear by unbalanced *taking*.

A new world must have new foundations. An eternal foundation is not built as one whole—it is built lovingly stone by stone. Thus must man rebuild his world.

Once again read the Law of Love that our Father has given as a foundation to bring everlasting peace to his world of man—

RHYTHMIC BALANCED INTERCHANGE.

III

THE MEANING OF
UNIVERSAL ONENESS

"Everything that is, is of every other thing that is. All things in My universe are indissolubly united as one."

From *The Divine Iliad*

When we speak of oneness—or universality—or unity—or the One Thing of scientific terminology, I doubt if one in a thousand has the slightest idea of what those terms really mean. We are so accustomed to multiplicity of units of every conceivable kind in Nature that separateness and separability are fixed concepts in our thinking. Also our own individuality of so many human individuals makes it well nigh impossible to think of mankind as one man inseparable from other men. It is still more impossible to think of the whole universe as One Thing with not one separable part.

Nevertheless it is true of God's universe that there are not two separate or separable things in it. Likewise it is true that there are not two individual human bodies or two individual human Souls in the vast entirety of this universe.

It is difficult to look into the starry heavens and think of all those millions of stars as one star. Yet they are all so indissolubly bound together that any action or variation upon one is as much a part of every other one as any happening anywhere happens everywhere.

Everybody who is familiar with radio knows that a voice sounding in England can be recondensed into sound anywhere on the planet—but few realize that every such sound is universal in its extent, reaching to the farthermost star with as much certainty and precision as to the next city from its point of utterance.

The growing comprehension of this electric age makes it possible for moderns to understand that principle of universality which, except for a few mystics, the ancients could not comprehend. These few did understand it, however, for their illuminations into cosmic awareness gave them that all-knowing. To them alone, God's processes of creation are fully known. Such knowledge can never come through the senses until inspiration unfolds in man to a sufficient extent to enable him to see and hear with the eyes and ears of the Spirit within him what he sees and hears with the eyes and ears of his body.

When inspired man can interpret the effects recorded upon his senses into the cause of those effects, then he comprehends the omniscience, omnipresence and omnipotence of God. He then has knowledge, but not until.

The more we know how God's thinking processes take God's knowing of His one idea apart—give it form and body, with seeming multiplicity, separability and individuality, then void all of those qualities by merging them into the oneness from which they came for the purpose of repeating them eternally— the more we can understand that God alone IS—that every point in the universe is the same point—that every extension from any one point is as though there were but one dimensionless point in all the universe.

Consider the oneness of any part of God's idea, such as the calm ocean. Its unchanging stillness, unbroken by waves of motion which seemingly divide it into many measurable units, might be likened to the stillness of the one Light of God's unchanging knowing, unbroken by the thinking of that knowing into many seemingly changing and measurable parts. Upon that calm ocean there are no separate or separable units to give multiplicity or individuality to its oneness. There is nothing there which changes, nothing to measure. One could not put his finger anywhere upon it and return to locate that same point, for every point upon it anywhere is the same point. There is no everywhere in it, for there is *no extension* in it—nothing that is relative to any other thing— for there is no other thing in the ocean's oneness for it to be relative to. The ocean can be relative to the shore, for that is another idea, but the oneness of one idea cannot be relative to itself.

The moment the still balance of the ocean becomes extended to two unbalanced opposite conditions, the unchanging oneness becomes a changing multiplicity. The unity of the ocean-idea is divided into wave units of that idea. Separateness and separability come into seeming being when one can count oneness into infinity—where the measureless can be measured—where variation from oneness gives individuality to varying and changing units.

Wherever unity is manifested by infinite numbers of units, no two of those units are alike. Likewise, where one balanced equal pressure is divided into two opposite unbalanced pressures, motion becomes imperative for the purpose of seeking balance.

The import of this is the fact that all divisibility and multiplicity, all individuality, changing, measure, unbalance and disunity come from oneness— from *unity* itself. Furthermore, all of these qualities of separateness return to the oneness from which they came for the purpose of again expressing their separateness in infinite numbers of forever changing units.

That fact of the division and multiplication of the unity of God's *knowing* into the infinity of God's *thinking*—for taking His One Idea apart and expressing it as many parts—then putting all those parts together again into the unity from which they came—is the one dominant characteristic of Creation. That is what Creation is—many changing units of moving light-waves arising from the stillness of the one Light, then returning to that stillness for rebirth into light-waves of motion.

Consider another phase of separateness, changing, individuality and measurableness arising from the same ocean-idea as mists and vapors instead of waves.

The love principle of Nature is manifested by the giving of ocean to the heavens and the regiving of an equal amount by the heavens to the earth. Multiplicity, separateness, individuality and the variation of changing are manifested in the countless units of cloud forms, raindrops, brooks, creeks, rivers, waterfalls, torrents and other forms which manifest the idea of water when set in motion as an infinity of units.

Consider the individuality of brooks, rivers and other streams. Each has its separate form. No two are

alike. Their individuality is named by man as Stony
Creek, North Mountain Brook, Hudson River or
Niagara Falls. The forms of each unit of water thus
divided from its oneness are as different from each
other as every man is different from every other
man.

Consider, also, the fact that every raindrop, brook,
river and stream seeks the unity of the ocean from
which it came for the purpose of finding the balance
of that oneness in order that it can repeat its seeming
separateness.

In this manner, life springs from oneness to manifest one-half of the life cycle, and returns to oneness
as death to manifest the other half. That is the inviolate order of Nature. There is no other order. That is
the law of Nature. There is no other law than that
one of *rhythmic balanced interchange* between the
opposite halves of cycles which forever spring from
oneness to manifest oneness in multiple forms of individual expressions.

When we say that life of man flows through him
to manifest the idea of man as a part of the God-idea,
it is like saying that the ocean forever flows through
each brook and river to manifest the idea of the
ocean.

Whenever we say that man has a forever changing
body to manifest the idea of man, it is like saying

that the brook has a forever changing body to manifest the idea of the brook.

Likewise, when we say that our bodies live and die because they appear and disappear in cycles, it can likewise be said that the bodies of brooks and rivers appear from the mist, disappear into the oneness of their source and reappear from it in countless cycles of appearance, disappearance and reappearance.

We cannot see the bodies of brooks when they are mist of heavens, nor when they disappear into the oneness of their ocean source, but that does not mean that there is a discontinuance anywhere in their cycles.

Likewise, when man's body disappears from our sensed vision into the earth and heavens from which it formerly appeared as an assemblage of gases, liquids and solids, we think of that body as having discontinued. We say it is dead. Yet it will appear from that same oneness of earth and heavens into which it disappeared as the same kind of a complex body which has no resemblance whatsoever to the earth or heavens from which it sprang.

Every individual separate thing which appears from any unitary source, whether from space, seed, earth, ocean or sun, disappears into that same oneness to lose its identity in its unity, and as surely reappears from that same source to regain its identity as a mul-

97

tiple unity of that one. That, again, is God's law. That is the order in which Nature asserts its continuity. The wombs of Nature are also tombs. Rebirths arise from death. Earths and heavens interchange equally. What earth gives to heaven in one-half of a life cycle, heaven gives back to earth to complete the cycle.

Consider the earth. If you dig a shovel of it anywhere, it all seems the same, yet out of it have come, and gone, countless millions of many varieties of flowers, insects, birds, animals, vegetables and chemical compounds to become digested into the oneness of that shovel full of earth. Think of the marvelous colors of growing things; think of the perfumes of flowers, the sounds of insects or of animals which have come from that earth and have gone back into the oneness of its dust. Think of the noises of city streets and of industry. All these have come from that dust of earth and have returned to it as death, as the death half of their cycles for reborning as their opposite life half.

Consider the seed of the tree. In its oneness it is the whole tree, every leaf of it—no two leaves being alike—every branch and twig of it, the bark of it, and the spiral of its unfolding. Yet the finest microscope in the world could not find even one of those countless leaves which will unfold from that seed into the variformed chlorophyll greens that, likewise, could not be found in the seed.

Consider the sun itself. In its oneness of incandescent light is every unit of form in all this creating universe. All animal life and vegetable life is there, together with all mineral forms, forms of metals, of crystals, the ruby, diamond and sapphire. Throughout the immense bulk of the sun is as much a oneness of simulated light in its incandescent form as the earth is a oneness of simulated light in its condensed form.

Everything we know of in our familiar environment of earth comes from the sun to manifest the idea of creating things in countless individual units of each idea. Our senses recognize these forms. We give each one a name to recognize its individuality. We analyze each one and note its differences from every other one.

Consider all waves of the ocean as being extensions of the ocean; therefore all being extensions of each other. If each wave is an extension of every other wave, it therefore follows that every action taking place on any one wave is likewise taking place on every other wave.

As no two waves are alike, so likewise are no two actions alike. A powerful action may take place upon one wave such as the catastrophe of a steamship broken in two, while nothing extraordinary takes place upon any other wave, small or large, within miles of that catastrophe.

Yet it cannot be said that one wave of the ocean was guilty of sinking that great ship. Every wave of the entire ocean, small and large, near and far, was equally responsible for the sinking of that ship, for one wave could not be except that all other waves be.

Likewise, all men, being extensions of each other, are equally responsible for the actions of each and every other man. No man on earth can say, "I am innocent. I have done nothing to hurt anyone." Civilization is the sum total of all mankind's thinking. It is what every man has made it. Not even the unborn babe is exempt from guilt of the entirety of the world's criminal actions as well as he is glorified by the greatest of noble actions. Every act of every man either lifts or lowers all mankind, as every raindrop and rising mist either raises or lowers the entire ocean. The Hitlers, Mussolinis and Napoleons are the products of the same civilization as are geniuses such as Mozart, Beethoven, Wagner, Michelangelo, Leonardo da Vinci and Edison. When one man hurts the world, it is because hate is in the world as a product of man's thinking. No one could or would hurt another if love alone were in the world.

Not one man in all Creation, except Jesus, has manifested only love. The world of men hate and fear as well as love.

Everything in this solar system emerged from the sun to manifest its own individuality in countless units. It then returns to it to lose its individuality and separateness in the oneness from which it sprang. That which was hot incandescent formless light becomes the cool form of a meadow violet, or orchid of the swamp, or a rose in your garden. The oneness of earths and oceans comes from the oneness of the sun. Each is an extension of the sun just as all forms which emerge from their seed are extensions of their seed—as their seed are extensions of the sun.

This is a universe of One Thing—LIGHT—the still Light of God. All creating things in it are simulations of that Light expressed by motion. All variations of form in the universe are variations of motion. Variation of motion deceives the senses of man into believing in varied substances of varied things. There are no substances nor varied things.

Individuality, separateness, change, measure and form are due entirely to spiral light-waves which centrifugally extend from the sun and return to it centripetally to repeat the extension and retraction.

There are no separate things in the universe. There are no two of anything. The universe is wholly MIND, omnipotent, omniscient, omnipresent MIND.

That which we call vibrating waves of matter are but the electric recordings of God's knowing as manifested by His thinking.

God alone IS.

IV

UNIVERSALITY

"I am newly come from the high heavens bearing a gift of love to man, to tear away the veil which hides the radiant face of God. To extend to man knowledge of his God, so that man may know himself as an extension of the One Being of the Universe, is the purport of my message. Therefore, hear thou me, all peoples of all nations."

—From *The Divine Iliad.*

Who knows the meaning of oneness? Until one knows that meaning, one believes that he lives and dies as a separate person, not knowing of his universality as a part of the WHOLE of Creation.

The brook on the mountainside is an individual; its name is Laughing Waters. Everyone knows that individual on the mountainside, knows where to find it, knows its song of laughing waters, knows its form just as we know the form of John Jones and Susie Smith—as individuals. But that brook is being born and reborn forever and ever. Its individuality is a

103

continuous One, an Eternal One, an Immortal One. That brook is forever seeking the oneness from which it came for the purpose of again becoming that brook whose name is Laughing Waters.

It came from the ocean, it sought the heavens to find rest, and it returned to the ocean to express the individuality of the One from which it sprang, for the purpose of expressing the idea of water.

It is forever attached to the heavens. It never is separated from the heavens. It is not just a brook which begins on the mountainside. If it could think, it would think of itself as an individual brook; it would not realize that it is replenishing itself forever from the heavens to be forever reborn for the purpose of seeking the oneness from which it comes. Nor could it realize that it is repeating itself as an individual forever and forever only because of its inseparability from both the heavens and the sea.

We are all seeking that oneness and we are all seeking separateness in individuality, forever and forever. The greatest desire of man seems to be to retain his individuality. "I am John Jones; I live in Boston; my address is so and so. Will I always be John Jones? When I come back again, will I remember who I am? And when the play is finished on this planet, will I start again as John Jones? Will I keep my individuality?" That is the perpetual question of all mankind.

John Jones does not realize that he sprang from the eternal, immortal, ONE UNIVERSAL BEING, and is constantly being replenished by Him. John Jones, the individual, could not say, "Before Abraham was, I AM." He would not know what it meant. But John, knowing of his oneness with the One from Whom he sprang, and from the ever replenishing of that oneness from the light of the heavens—John Jones, knowing the rhythm of his body as something which is flowing out of him and into him all the time, unfolding and refolding from light of sun and earth—never being the same for a moment,—that John Jones could say, "Before Abraham was, I AM," and he would know what it meant. To be a great individual is to know how to lose one's life in order to find it—to die sequentially in order to be sequentially reborn.

Every thought is a cycle. One half of each cycle is away from God toward separateness; the other equal half is back toward God to oneness. Each action of life is the fulfillment of the law of the two opposite desires of God to manifest in units and multiplicity as individuals drawing their power from God, knowing of their relationship with God—and then returning to God in every thought cycle as in every life cycle. In thinking, we concentrate to manifest God by building form images which are conceived first in the Mind of God and then extended through the Mind of man in form images created by man's co-creating with God. We must decentrate to conceive and then concentrate to create form of our concepts.

When we can do that, we can say, "Before Abraham was, I AM." We can also say, "I AM the son of God," and know its meaning. We can then say it with authority and know that we are one with God. Men who can knowingly say this are great individuals—and there are but few of them—one in millions. On the face of the earth today, 999,999 of every million do not know it. They do not know of their immortality as sons of God. They are the individuals who wish to retain their individuality, hug it, nurse it, not knowing from whence their power comes—not knowing that separable units of any idea of God's Creation are impossible.

In this new age, we must have more of such universal men. The cosmic age is coming into being. This is the age in which we shall know God, know His nature in order that we may obey His laws. The message of The Divine Iliad is a cosmic message of power for all who are going out into the world to manifest Oneness through multiplicity.

The way to be a creative individual is to know that each person is an inseparable extension of the One Great Individual. Never lose sight of that for a moment. Do not pray morning, noon and night at timed intervals. Let your prayers be continuous, from moment to moment. To know God is to be God. To know God, one must decentrate—which means to stop thinking to lose one's individuality in Oneness with God. For each *decentrated* thought goes to the Source to bring back the *concentrated* expression of it for the purpose of being a great individual by knowing one's immortal Self as an extension of God.

The Divine Iliad is a message to the New Age—to the new race which will spring from new knowing of God—of the laws of Nature—and of the relationship of man to God, not as separate units of the man-idea but as unity—as wholeness—oneness—inseparable oneness. Within the message is the secret of Light. God is Light. Light is all that IS. To know the secret of Light is to know all things.

Immortality manifests immortality. But when we leave out immortality and manifest only mortality, we are weaklings. We have been weaklings for too many centuries—too many long centuries. Let us grow up; let us awaken into the Light of our New Day! Let the spiritual be reborn in us. Let us rise above our sensing and know that we are extensions of the ONE Source—then let us manifest that Source in power.

V

ARE WE REALLY ALIVE?

There is much confusion concerning Life and the Life Principle. In animate beings, we generally think of the Life Principle as the pulsing heartbeat—so we say that bodies live when the heart is beating and that they die when the heart stops beating.

The fact is that bodies neither live nor die. Bodies express life, but the expression of life is not Life. Life is in the one still motionless Light of the Creator Himself, and is expressed in bodies as an extension of life evidenced in Nature. The Creator alone lives as the One Universal Being. The Creator is LIGHT—one still Light of all-knowing. Creation is God's knowing expressed by His thinking.

The whole creating universe, therefore, is but a pulsing electric record of God's thinking expressed by electric waves of motion. Man's body is, therefore, but states of motion which record the idea of man as one part of the whole idea of creation. Waves of motion cannot know anything, nor can they live or die. Waves belong to the electric universe which manifests God's idea in forms of that idea, but the body itself thus expressed is not the idea. The idea is never created; it remains forever in the Mind of the Creator.

This brings us face to face with the fact that the body is not the Person or Self of man. The Self of man is God in man. God is the One Universal Being. The One Being alone lives. The One Being alone is eternal and immortal.

The body of man is eternally repetitive. It forever appears, disappears, and reappears in cycles, just as everything else in Nature appears, disappears and reappears in cycles. We call the cycles of man's appearance and disappearance life and death; but bodies, never having lived, cannot die. *There is no death in all the universe. There is but a continual repetition of life cycles of rebirth into their two opposite expressions which we call life and death, but both are, in fact, one.*

It is this supposition that the person is the body, and that the body lives and dies, that causes man to think that bodies are realities when, in fact, all reality is in the Spirit which centers man—that core of identity by which each individual knows himself as "I." That "I" of the individual person is not in the body. It can never disappear. The "I" is eternal—it is immortal.

It will simplify our comprehension of the nature of the universe to realize that all we have got to deal with in the entire universe is Light—the one Light of God, the Creator, and the two lights of God's thinking which is electrically recorded as matter and space. These two opposite expressions are represented by incandescent light of the sun and the black light of space. Our bodies are composed of electric waves of those two lights interwoven into forms just as the tapestry weaver weaves forms into fabric.

Bodies of all creating things are merely the electric product of Mind-thinking, expressing Mind-knowing. It is not logical to conceive of any electrically-manufactured product as living or dying. Even though it is a human body, it is as much a product of God's thinking as the automobile is a product of man's thinking. We never think of the automobile as "living," even though it expresses power and motion and has the heartbeat of the electric current which activates it. We know that the Intelligence which manifests life, power and motion in that car is in the Intelligence which operates it and is not in the car itself.

The sooner we can realize that our bodies are as much machines which obey the will of the Intelligence which operates them, as all of men's machines likewise are, the more we will look to that centering

Intelligence of man as the reality. We must some day realize that the body is but an instrument which periodically wears out and has to be replaced just as automobiles wear out and have to be replaced.

What we have said of the Life Principle is true also of knowledge and power. We think of knowledge and power as qualities which belong to our bodies. Knowledge and power are also cosmic qualities which are in God only. Our bodies know nothing, nor have they the power to lift even one finger without reaching for that knowledge or power through the electric cables of light which extend from the still Light of God to the moving light-waves which our bodies are.

Waves of water extend from the calm sea. Waves of water manifest the power of the sea, but that power is not in the waves of motion but in the still sea itself. That power is in the sea whether manifested by waves or not.

Likewise, our bodies are light-waves of motion extended from the stillness of the One Light within which is all power, all knowledge and all presence. Knowledge and power are, therefore, but manifested in the light-waves of motion which our bodies are; but they, themselves, have no knowledge or power, just as they have no life or death.

The belief that our bodies are ourselves leads us,

also, to believe that our bodies think and that our brains do our thinking. This, also, is not true. Our brains are but electric storehouses for memories recorded upon them as a result of the experiences of our senses. They are, also, the nerve center of all parts of the body just as a switchboard is the nerve center of multiple extensions. Without that switchboard, the distant parts of the body could not make the rest of the body aware of their condition, nor could any part of the body act to express the will of its centering Intelligence.

The will to act is not in the body, however. It, too, is in the centering Intelligence which operates the body; and that centering Intelligence is the God-Self which man is. The will to act is in the Person, the Being, which man is. It is not in the body.

Gradually, man emerges from his primate jungle abode to the high mountain top of his divine inheritance. The farther he is removed from his early beginnings and the more he is extended into the Light of all knowing, the more he becomes aware of that God-Self which motivates his body, and the more he relies upon it instead of his body.

For this reason, man gradually becomes co-creator with God by constant intercommunication with God through the language of Light which man knows as inspiration. Inspiration is man's direct intercommunication with God. It is the basis of all genius. It is the answer to the difference between the average man and the rare mystic.

Look ye, therefore, to the Light within you and not to the body with which you but manifest that Light; for in that is your only way to power, and that only way is toward God, the Source of all things, without Whom nothing in this universe could be or become.

VI

GENIUS INHERENT IN EVERYONE

I shall read to you from *THE DIVINE ILIAD*. I wish these words to be burned into your consciousness because they are fraught with much meaning.

"*Man is Light when he knows that he is Light. Through My Light alone can man know Me.*

"*To know Me is to be Me.*

"*When man knows the Light which binds all things to Me, he is then ONE with Me.*

"*Behold in Me the One, inseparable.*

"*Two things there are not in MY universe. There is but one.*

"*Everything that is, is of every other thing that is. Nothing is of itself alone. All things are indissolubly united.*

"*This is a universe of seeming; an imaged universe of thinking; an action universe of desiring. That which Mind desires will appear in the image of that desire.*

"*Desire ye what ye will and, behold, it standeth*

before thee. Throughout the aeons it has been thine
without thy knowing, e'en though thou hast but just
asked for it.

"Sit ye not and ask, acting not, for thy desire will
not come thy way to thee unaided by thy strong
arms.

"Behold, I am within all things centering them;
and I am without all things controlling them, but I
am not those things which I center in them and con-
trol in space surrounding them.

"I am the center of My universe of Me. Every-
where I am is the center of all things, and I am ev-
erywhere."

It is my desire to correct the commonly accepted
misconception regarding the idea that geniuses are
specially born. By genius, I mean that quality of Consciousness possessed by such outstanding geniuses as
Rubens, Leonardo, Titian and Raphael; such philosophers as Socrates, Plato, Marcus Aurelius, Plotinus,
Laotzu and Confucius; such mystics as Buddha, Moses, Mohammed, Baha'u'llah, and the supreme mystic of all time, Jesus the Nazarene. Also our modern
geniuses such as Beethoven, Mozart, Chopin, Rachmaninoff, Paderewski, Edison, Marconi, and their
prototypes which are altogether too few in these
thousands of years of world history. None is so rare

among men as a genius. Out of hundreds of millions, we have but one.

Go down through the pages of history and count them. You can put them all on a very small page. From these few, the culture of our race and its very resurrection from the jungle has come. These few have been our path to our ultimate mountain top. Our awareness of our very souls has come to us from these few who first found God in themselves and extended their awareness to each one of us in the measure of our ability to receive that awareness.

And even more rare are the mystics—one in billions or even in tens of billions.

Is it any wonder, then, that people say "geniuses are born as geniuses, and there is no hope for us." I do not blame people who say that. I do not wonder when people ask: "Is there any hope for me?" I do not wonder when parents discourage their children who wish to be important in the world and say, "There is no genius in our family—no great musician —no inventor. We are just everyday people. Why are you wasting your time? Go get a job." And that happens thousands and thousands of times as parents pull children down—inspired children who begin to know the Light in themselves—who recognize the Light in themselves. Desire is keen in young people at such awakenings. It is a great crime for parents to strip the very souls of their children when they thus hear the Inner Voice of the Light and wish to manifest it.

We all inherit *all* that God has to give. The maximum of genius is in everyone. A spoonful is not given to one and a bowlful to another and a bushel to another. We are all born equal in the Light of God. We are His omniscient Light, and all of it centers in us. The only difference between the greatest genius in the world and the ordinary man is that the genius is aware of the Light within him and the ordinary man is not aware of that Light. The omnipotent Light is in everyone—all of it—in all of its fullness. Likewise, all knowledge is in the Light of everyone, awaiting one's awareness of it.

Light is the Self and Soul of everyone; the omniscient, omnipotent and omnipresent Light which is God. That Light of all-knowing is the foundation of Creation. It is the One still Light from which the two moving lights of this electric universe spring to manifest the One. Gradually, and all too slowly, we become aware of the Light of our Soul-Selves. We have been out of the jungle for only a few thousands of the millions of years of man's unfolding. We are in the infancy of the human race—the wonder is that so many have become aware of even so much.

Do not include among so-called geniuses the men

of great information who have given us discoveries based upon research and observation. Those men are no greater in knowledge than the ancient men who discovered the flame, the wheel, the boat and the sail for the boat. They are greater only in their greater amount of information and their skills gained from greater powers of observation and will to work. All *material* civilization has grown from a *material* standpoint. The early discoverers of the boat, the sail, the wheel and the plane were but keen observers of material phenomena. More specialized observation, research and reasoning from such observation has brought us to where we are now.

We have but multiplied our power of observation of material phenomena. While thus multiplying our ability to observe, we have multiplied our reasoning and thinking powers and our skills for the purpose of learning how to put more things together and take them apart.

While learning the HOW, we have never learned the WHY or WHAT. That is why science today has so little knowledge of CAUSE. It produces effects but cannot tell the WHY of those effects.

The greatest living scientists do not know what electricity is; nor can they define gravitation, magnetism, light, life, energy, nor the construction of matter. Their theories in these respects are but wild guesses which are so often changed that scientific textbooks become obsolete in a few years. For that reason, the world of today is well *informed* with observed effects and skills in the use of materials but has practically no *knowledge*.

Effects of motion cannot be *known* because they are transient, changing, evanescent things. They can but be comprehended. Knowledge lies in CAUSE, and until we know *cause* in the *why* of things, we have no knowledge.

Where are we today? Information and skills have put us where we are now, not knowledge. Knowledge is the omnipotent, omnipresent and omniscient Light. That Light is within everyone and everything to its fullest extent. It is in every cell of one's body, centering it. It is in the magnetic poles of everyone, controlling them. You may have that Light of all-knowledge for the asking. Knowledge is cosmic; it is universal. Desire what you will of it and it will unfold within you. You will suddenly become consciously aware of it by receiving a flash of inspiration. That flash is your answer.

We are what we desire to be. We can be what we wish to be. If we make a plan of our own lives and desire that plan to be fulfilled, we will become *that*. And all the laws of the universe will help us to become that. Each step in the unfoldment of desire leads to new unfoldment.

Desire to be great and you will be. Desire to kill

and you can also kill. The universe helps equally in either case. The universe works with each person to help him fulfill his desire, no matter what that desire is. We can make or break ourselves. Our lives are our own making. If we work with the law of balance, we achieve balanced results. If we break the law, the law breaks us to an equal extent—and immediately.

I often say to groups, especially the salesmen's groups to whom I have talked for many years: "*Mediocrity is self inflicted; genius is self bestowed.*" Take your choice. It lies with you. A genius is one who is conspicuously aware of the Light in him; one who lives in the balanced rhythms of the God Light. A genius is a co-creator with God. He is the bridge between man and God. The geniuses of the world give us our culture. They uplift mankind.

A mystic is one who is more fully aware of the Light. He is the supreme genius. Jesus, the one mystic of all time, can never be exceeded, but he can be equaled. The end of the journey of man is to equal Jesus in full cosmic consciousness of the Light.

On one of these evenings, I will tell you the story of the journey of man from the jungle to the Light. All mankind will eventually have full conscious awareness of the Light whether he will or not. Even though he walks toward the dark, he must eventually turn and go the other way. He has no choice in the matter. When he has sufficiently punished himself by walking toward the dark, he will turn to ease his own self-inflicted suffering. Each one of us is walking either toward the dark or the Light.

The decision as to which way you walk is under your control. You are either seeking God or trying to escape from Him. The genius or mystic who has found God lives in the world of inspiration. He is always seeking the ecstasy of the Light. He lives in that wonderful ecstatic world of aloneness, and prefers to. He is never alone—for he is with God—thinking God—creating with God.

He is forever interpreting the inspiration of God's whisperings to him, whether they be in musical rhythms, inventions, poetry or sculpture, or any product of industry. Every man who is inspired to manifest God worthily is expressing the measure of his own genius, whether he manifests it in the kitchen, in the workshop, or in running an elevator. One who is joyously and ecstatically working to the best of his ability to manifest God in him is expressing the genius in him. He is the one who is walking toward the Light—the one who is trying to be worthy of the Light.

The one who is walking away from God is he who does not wish to be alone. He is afraid to be alone with God; he is afraid to be alone for fear he will run into God. He fears inspiration; he fears the Inner Voice speaking to him. If the Inner Voice ever so much as gets in a little word, he turns on the radio to drown it out. And if the music is not quick enough, he will seek for jazz, speeches or advertising. He will turn the dial here, and back again—change from one place to another—turn it off and go out for a card game—go to a bar room to drink and seek pleasure for the body in company with other bodies like him. Such a man is not seeking God; he is trying to escape from God. Such a man is not walking toward genius. He uses every effort to find a way to get away from God the moment he finds himself in danger of being alone with his Self.

The genius is just the opposite. He seeks the forest, the quietude of Nature; he seeks good music—good literature—uplifting things. The great creator Rachmaninoff multiplies himself by dividing himself and giving himself and those divided parts to the whole world for its uplift. The one who is walking away from God divides himself by himself. That is the seed he sows for which he reaps the harvest of mediocrity and failure to achieve eternal values.

You who sit in an audience and hear Rachmaninoff, and say, "Geniuses must be born," or "there is no genius in me,"—or hear the music of Tschaikovsky or Beethoven—or any of the music which has the rhythms of heaven in it—the rhythms which make you forget your body as the composer forgot his body when he created it—you who feel thrills up and down your spine while you listen to it are a mirror which is reflecting that genius. His inspiration is being reflected in you. You are being re-inspired by him, and that is the evidence of your genius whether you perform it or not, or whether you have ever done anything in your life to express genius.

When you are thus inspired by another, you are multiplying your Self by *knowingly* becoming one with other Selves. You are unifying your Soul with the universal Soul through your increasing awareness of the universal Soul.

The very fact of its reflection in you is evidence of your own inner genius. You love it, and you walk alone afterward to be in the ecstatic aftermath of that wonderful harmony. For days it keeps recurring to you, whispering the reflection of cosmic rhythms back to you. For days they pulse in your heart and become a part of you, a permanent part of you. It is as though they said to you, "Be me. I am the Light." *The music you heard was the Inner Voice of the Light. It was the door to the Light through which you can enter.* Wherever you hear good music or see good art— wherever you are inspired by anything whatsoever— and uplifted by it to any extent whatsoever—you are walking toward your own genius in the Light and away from mediocrity.

However, the fruit of genius does not drop into one's lap. One cannot be a wishful thinker, sitting idly waiting for the material manifestation of one's thought.

All the great geniuses I have known have certain traits in common, and not the least of these is a great capacity for work. They find inspiration in their great reverence for Nature and a deep desire to be alone. Their awareness of God is born in "aloneness" with Self.

Personal contact with such men as Paderewski, Leopold Godowsky, George Gershwin, Ossip Gabrilowitsch, Victor Herbert, John Philip Sousa, Caruso and others among musicians; with Coolidge, Shapley, Michaelson, Millikan, Jeans, Edison and others of the great scientists and inventors—was living proof to me that these men had unfolded their genius because of their cooperation with God.

In their oneness with the Source, they became immune from fatigue and their inner awareness is portrayed in a seemingly unlimited personal power of accomplishment.

Likewise, I, too, found the kingdom of heaven within me. Since the age of seven I have consciously walked and talked with God. Whatever I have created has been co-created with God, in that ecstasy of Mind which is the unchanging nature of God. Whatever I have achieved is because of the awareness of God working with me as One Mind—achieving through me as One Thinker—not two or three times a day—before and after meals by saying prayers periodically in words—but continuously—consciously, moment by moment.

I do not think I have ever prayed in words. I pray in conscious desire. I pray in concepts—concepts of whole ideas, not parts. I never go to sleep at night without consciously thinking that kind of prayer in which I express desire in whole ideas of what my day for the morrow must be. I do not weaken my prayer by trying to find words for it. I keep my desire strong by not thus dividing it into words or in parts. My prayers are communions, not conversations.

The night is the most important part of life. We waste our precious nights through not knowing what sleep means, and what it is that sleeps. Certainly it is not Consciousness which sleeps. It is also certain that there is no such state as unconsciousness. We must know that in order that we may make use of our nights to hasten our journey to our mountain top and not be limited to the day alone.

The day is for thinking and acting; the night is for gaining new knowledge and inspiration for manifesting God in a masterly way. If our thinking is an extension of Light within us, our creations are masterpieces—and they must be because God does not fail us when He inspires us with His mighty rhythms.

God does not allow mediocrity to pass through us when the ecstasy of our thinking reflects the ecstasy of His thinking. The wholeness of God's knowing and the rhythm of His ecstasy within us makes us forget all time—forget all body—forget everything but the Spirit within us. By so thinking, we unfold our genius. In like manner, we revitalize our bodies through the inner joyousness of Mind which insulates the body from toxins engendered by fears, worries, and the boredom of monotony. All who desire to thus awaken their inherent genius may do so by thus desiring to awaken it.

"How can I acquire cosmic consciousness?" people ask. "How can I become cosmically educated, as you have?" I have often been asked to tell of my illumination into that rare state of knowing which is known as Cosmic Consciousness. I have not formally attended school or a university since the age of nine, but have had a super-university education and training purely from the Cosmos by walking and talking with God.

Beginning at the age of seven, I have experienced cosmic illumination every May. For ten days or more during these periods, I had to seek aloneness in the forest. The essence of these illuminating experiences was recorded by me and will soon be published as "The Book of Early Whisperings."

Every seventh year these illuminations were very intense. In the seven times seventh year—at forty nine—came the greatest of these periodic illuminations. It was at that time that the cosmic state of all-knowing remained with me for thirty-nine days and nights. During those thirty-nine days of illumination "The Divine Iliad" was written. This divinely inspired cosmic message was given by our Father so that man could transform himself through new comprehension of His still Light and His electric-wave universe of moving light.

Many people desire cosmic illumination at its fullest, as the great mystics have experienced it. This rare experience is very dangerous because it is very difficult for the severed Consciousness to again function in the body by normal coordination of sensation and Consciousness.

The best way to acquire the Light is to become aware of it gradually. Seek it by desiring it. New awareness and comprehension will then slowly awaken in you as the Inner Voice awakens you through inspiration.

It is better to be gradually transformed as the

whole human race marches toward the mountain top than to have it all at once and suffer the crucifixion and aloneness of being ahead of your time and waiting long, patient years in which you may not even speak of it.

  *"Man is forever seeking the Light to guide him on that long, tortuous road which leads from his body's jungle to the mountain top of his awakening Soul. Man is forever finding that Light and is being forever transformed as he finds it; and as he finds it, he gradually finds the Self, which is the Light. And as he becomes more and more transformed by the God Light of the awakening Self within him, he leaves the jungle farther behind him in the dark from which he is being released by his gradual transformation from the electric awareness of the Spirit.

  "There are those who seek the Light who are discouraged because they seemingly cannot find it, being wholly unaware that they have been forever finding it. Unknowing ones expect to find it all at once in some blinding flash, revealing all power, all knowledge and all Presence. It does not come that way until one is nearing his mountain top. Man cannot bear too much of the Light at a time while his body is still

* Quoted from "The Secret of Light."

new. It is too near its jungle to bear the Light. All who are well out of the jungle have already found enough of the Light to illumine their way out of the depths. They are forever finding all they can bear. He who is far out of the jungle and still seeks the Light in the high heavens is forever finding it, and is forever being transformed as he finds it.

"The dark road from man's jungle to his mountain top glory becomes ever more illumined during the ascent of man from his body to the Spirit. It is a hard but glorious road to climb. All must make it.

"The ascent of man from the dark to the Light is the forever repetitive play which man is playing on this planet.

"When all mankind has found the Light, the play will be finished; likewise this planet will be finished as its abode for men. It will then be rolled off into its ever-expanding orbit where Venus is gradually being rolled into place to become the stage for the next repetition of the ascent of man in the solar system.

"We actors of the play must, therefore, be content with the lines of the play revealed to us each moment in life. We must likewise be ever joyous at our continuous transformation bit by bit, moment by moment, from day to day and from year to year. And each one of us learns his part line by line, the better to fulfill them worthily.

"All parts of the play manifested by man are experiences which become actions of the play. All experiences are part of man's unfolding; each a part of his journey from the dark to the Light which constitutes the play. All experiences are steps in man's journey from the jungle to man's mountain top of glory. All experiences, therefore, are good experiences. There is naught but good; there is no evil. There is naught but life, there is no death."

I shall end where I began, by reminding you in burning words from *THE DIVINE ILIAD* which I wish to recall for your own salvations:

"Man is Light when he knows that he is Light. Through My Light alone can man know Me.

"To know Me is to be Me.

"When man knows the Light which binds all things to Me, he is then ONE with Me."

VII

THINK

The subject of my last talk to you was entitled "Genius Inherent in Everyone." Today I will talk to you regarding the mental training of geniuses in all walks of life, the secret of their achievements, their philosophies of life and the experiences they must pass through in order to attain a high goal of success.

I believe all people are messengers of the Universal One, born here on earth to manifest God in them. We are all actors in the divine drama which is unfolding day by day and making civilization what the Creator intends that it shall be. It is from that high point of view that I am approaching this subject of genius, and by genius I mean the super-thinking salesman, lawyer, inventor or craftsman, as well as the great artistic geniuses.

The subject of my talk will be the one word THINK. It is the only word in a one-word slogan used by Thomas J. Watson, President of International Business Machines Corporation. That one word THINK is in every room of every office and factory in the 79 countries where that great organization functions.

The text of my subject is from *THE DIVINE ILIAD:* "*ALL that God hath, He giveth me; He withholdeth nothing.*" By that I mean that all intelligence, knowledge and power are the divine inheritance of every one. Those who become aware of their unlimited mental power climb above all others up the ladder of creative thinking. Others merely absorb the thinking of their fellowmen into the sensed machines of their electric bodies and act like automatons repeating the thoughts and actions of others like parrots.

The popular conception of a genius is that of a rare super-being to whom qualities have been given which have been denied to the ordinary run of men. The average man looks up to the genius, but never hopes to attain his level.

We often think of God that way, as though He were an extraneous Being that we may look up to from afar, but never see and never know. If I could not feel that I know God and am a part of God, I would feel that life was not worth living. Or if I knew that I could not earn my divine inheritance of genius, I would feel that hope, itself, is a useless thing.

If you do not think that genius is within you, then your life would be as empty and as hopeless as it would be if you also felt that you could not in any manner comprehend God or God's presence in Nature.

The idea that genius is reserved for the few and not for all is a fallacy. Genius is within everyone who thinks. It is a product of Mind, and the completeness of Mind is universal in all beings through which it flows in thought-forms.

Webster says: "To think is to exercise the mind actively in any way."

The genius is described as one "having exalted and phenomenal intellectual power and creative ability."

The great geniuses who have given us our standards of civilization have not exceeded three hundred in number since the beginning of this age, out of the millions and millions of people who have been born.

Among the world's thinkers, there is one greater and far more rare than the genius. He is known as the mystic. So rare is he that one hardly concedes his possible present-day existence, for, since the beginning of history, hardly thirty mystics have been born out of the countless millions of the world's people.

A mystic is defined by Webster as "One who relies chiefly upon meditation in acquiring truth." He defines mysticism as "The doctrine or belief that man may obtain immediate consciousness or knowledge of God."

Every genius is to some extent a mystic, but the true mystic has a Consciousness of his unity with God to such an extent that the invisible spiritual universe is as perceptible to him as the material universe is to the ordinary man.

The ecstatic state of "Cosmic Consciousness" is the term given to that type of thinking which is common to the mystic. Jesus is known as the greatest of mystics. Mystics are the super-thinkers of civilization who have attained greatest knowledge and greatest power.

Each one of us gradually becomes aware of the genius or mystic in us by that Silent Voice whispering within each one of us. In the measure of our ability and willingness to listen to the inspiring rhythms which flow through us as direct messages flashed from the Universal Mind are we approaching the genius or the mystic.

Mr. Watson knew that he could create a super-organization of supermen only by increasing their thinking power by inspiring them with greater knowledge and comprehension. He also knew that very few people "THINK" at all and that is why civilization is at such a low standard.

Each person feels quite certain that he *thinks*,

but not one in a hundred really does think. He is merely obeying automatic reflexes inherited through millions of repeated lives.

Mr. Watson knew that people could be taught to think, even to the point of developing the latent genius which is within every man. That is why he posted that auto-suggestive word "THINK" everywhere throughout his organization, and then instituted certain orderly procedures which compelled his men to think.

For this reason and for his vision which is evolving a higher standard of manhood, I believe Thomas J. Watson to be one of the world's greatest geniuses, one who has contributed much to the pattern of our American civilization.

Just as Leonardo, Michelangelo, Beethoven, Shakespeare, and other geniuses gave us our older culture, so have five Americans predominated in preparing our American civilization for a higher culture and ethical code than we have ever known.

Five Americans whom I believe have made priceless contributions to this New Age which we are about to enter are: George Washington, Abraham Lincoln, Mary Baker Eddy, Thomas A. Edison and Thomas J. Watson.

George Washington and Abraham Lincoln wove the pattern of our present civilization and our present idea of a democracy of free men which both lived and fought for—which Lincoln so powerfully expressed in his Gettysburg speech. Thomas Jefferson, Tom Paine and Benjamin Franklin were the nucleus of a group of great Americans who interwove the idea of freedom into its present pattern.

Mary Baker Eddy was the first one in this New Age to remind growing civilization that this is a mental universe.

Mary Baker Eddy was a mystic. She prepared the way for the cooperation of science and religion to open long-closed doors of thought into the New Age which will build a new concept of God in accordance with the new comprehension which this electric age has given us. For this conspicuous service, the ages will owe her an incalculable debt of gratitude.

Edison helped to prepare that new comprehension. As you all know, I made a portrait bust of him and very often, when I was working with him, I could see the light in his eyes that proclaimed him to me a super-genius, bordering on the mystic. He told me that everything he had ever invented or thought of came to him in timeless flashes.

All mystics describe their revelations as coming to them in flashes of great light. Paul, Buddha, Isaiah, Baha'u'llah and other mystics have vividly described this mental experience to such an extent that in the old days that experience was known as "The Illumination."

That experience is, in reality, a severance of the cosmic seat of Consciousness from the electric seat of sensation. The brain feels that severance electrically as a blinding flash. The Consciousness, thus freed from sensation, suddenly becomes cosmically aware of *cause* instead of being hampered by the sensation of effect. That is what is meant by the Biblical statement *"And ye shall know all things."*

Edison, building upon foundations laid by Franklin and Faraday, prepared the way for a new comprehension of this electric universe so that we know that anything which happens anywhere, happens everywhere. He prepared the way for our present radio-consciousness which gives us a new concept of energy and of the universe in general.

Jesus could not talk about the universality of all happenings although He knew all *cause*. The comprehension of people in His day would not permit it.

Jesus was the consummate scientist. He knew the omnipresence of Light which we have expressed in radio, radar and television, but all He could say in His day was: *"I have yet many things to say unto you, but ye cannot bear them now."*

Thomas A. Edison contributed more to elevate man to the new electric awareness than any other scientist or inventor, for he laid the groundwork for practically all of our greatest electrical progress.

Thomas Watson is laying the groundwork for greater international solidarity, thus doing more toward stabilizing civilization in preparation for a new social one-world order than any other living man. What Washington and Lincoln did politically to bring world freedom and the brotherhood-of-man into being, he is doing economically.

He is sowing the seed of a neighborly internationalism which will mark the next great step in the evolution of civilization. As a race, we are hardly out of that tribal stage in which wars are imperative. Neighborly internationalism will make wars impossible. A close study of the international family unity, mutuality and inter-racial friendliness of this world-girdling legion of men—all working for a common purpose—will reveal the leavening effect of a mighty force working silently against the possibility of mutual destruction and conspicuously in the direction of mutual construction.

What the churches and other cultural organizations are doing *religiously and ethically* to uplift the race, Mr. Watson is doing *practically* by demonstrating Truth in *practice* rather than in *theory*. Under the guise of an industrial organization, he is demonstrating brotherly love, unity, justice, cooperation and all the qualities which uplift men from mediocrity to genius, and from irresponsibility to responsibility, throughout the world.

The International Business Machines Corporation is not just a great money-making business; it is a world-wide man-making institution which is lifting the whole standard of human thought toward a higher pinnacle.

New ethical principles heretofore unknown in business practice have bound this great international body together as one great family which is as operative under any system of government as it is in the capitalistic system under which it now operates.

Our bodies were made in the same way that this organization was built—by adding thought by thought to it during all time.

Consider our own beginning millions of years before we were what we are now—a single protoplasmic cell upon which the light shone. When the light of the sun shines upon the seed of God's idea, it polarizes that idea into a manifestation of life, for the light is the Life messenger from space. All matter consists of light-waves and man is matter. Every particle of our body is light polarized into pulsating life by light-wave messengers from space. When light shone upon our single cell and polarized it, sensation was born into it. Desire for better and bigger bodies eventually made us what we are.

That was the process of the creation of your body

by the Universal Intelligence gradually working out the idea of the body of man as extension of desire. In this universe, nothing is created without the desire for creation. So, gradually, cellular forms were added to our bodies—our arms, our legs, our finger nails, and all the organs, nerves and veins which made us into the very complex automatic machines that we are today.

As we grew and unfolded our patterns, each added particle was connected with every other particle by a sensitized nerve so that each added part automatically took care of itself. To this sensed nerve was added an electric connection with every other part of the body so that eventually there grew up with each body a series of automatic reflexes, such as my standing here automatically balanced by reflexes which do not require me to think in order to stand. Automatically I stand here balanced, automatically my heart beats. As the body has grown, part by part, muscles, sinews, sensed nerves and electric flux were directly connected with the brain from which they got their driving power as directed by the Universal Intelligence which *consciously* manifests through the brain. Be it understood, however, that the brain of the body is not the *Intelligence* of the person who inhabits the body.

Automatic reflexes make it possible for us to do

about ninety-nine per cent of the things we do with about one per cent of thought energy expended. The Mind is free to create patterns for ideas and make decisions for our actions, for upon those decisions and actions lie the success or failure of our lives.

It would be well to illustrate the process of acquiring automatic reflexes by calling to your attention the tireless repetition of the musician, painter, sculptor, or of anyone who must make his body work automatically and leave his Mind free for thinking his knowledge into form.

Consider the pianist as he painfully thinks each separate note of a chord, then plays it unmusically until his body automatically senses whole bars at a time through his eyes, while his Mind is free to think the interpretation of his inspiration.

The salesman or craftsman must go through the same training in order that his body may act automatically and not sidetrack his Mind-power from its creative purpose.

This training imparts a memory to every cell of the body, for every cell added to a body has a purpose, and it "remembers" its purpose. Likewise, each part has a purpose and is reminded of it, and trained for it by the electric extensions which reach from the brain to each cell and part. Thus the fingers which have been added to the body for the mechanical purpose are as much trained into becoming automatons for the fulfilling of their purpose as a regiment of men trained to act in unison will fulfill their purpose as a unit. The salesman whose brain alone is trained parrot-like to act in accordance with his technical business education is merely a parrot or a robot. He repeats almost automatically the things he has been trained to repeat by the impressions made upon his brain alone. Such training does not develop THINKERS.

Now, it must be known that the brain of a man is not his Mind. *Mind is cosmic.* The brain is the focal point of the Universal Consciousness which centers millions of brains for repetition, just as any expression of Idea which is given back to the Cosmos condenses within millions of radios for repetition.

The brain is merely a seat of sensations and a storage place for the electric patterns of ideas which we call memories of events, which have taken place since our beginnings and, also, for the patterns of ideas which we have stored up as knowledge.

The brain does not think. It merely acts electrically according to the direction of the Consciousness. And it acts only when it is being charged by the universal electric force. That charging process continues for about three-quarters of a day and then gives way to a discharging process which we call sleep. The Conscious Intelligence, however, does not sleep or fatigue. It is merely the electrically-recording brain which sleeps or fatigues, thus disconnecting the brain from the Universal Intelligence temporarily.

This fact every genius knows as he knows his alphabet, and this knowledge governs every moment of his life, night and day. He never loses sight of this fact for one moment, for he knows that the penalty of an unbalanced action is an unbalanced body, and the consequent insulation of Mind from body instead of acquiring the freedom of Mind which allows the body to function automatically.

Consider the contrasting thought of the average badly-trained wise-cracking salesman who thinks he may do what he chooses on his own time, even to getting drunk and so incapacitating his body that he is unable to do any creative thinking for days.

I recall the reply of one of Mr. Watson's salesmen who, when I spoke to him about doing something for me on his own time, said, "I have no time of my own. All of my time belongs to the organization. Also all of my time is my own."

What did he mean? He meant that no man who is working out a great idea is free at any time to do anything which he knows he should not do. If he has an important thing to do the next day, the thing that he does that night has an influence upon the next day's success. If he carouses, drinks, or spends his time in any unbalancing pursuit, thereby lowering the vitality of his body, or lowers the tempo of the rhythm which flows through him, he incapacitates himself for the next day to the extent in which he has insulated Mind from his body. By so doing, he has not only stolen the time of the organization but stolen his own time. He has delayed his own success and lowered the standard of his entire organization by just that measure of his unbalanced act.

Each man is searching for Self, trying to find that within him which is the higher Self, the Essence of his own immortality.

The young man who is making his way in life, who prates much of free will and thinks that there is a certain time he is going to work for his boss and a certain time he is going to do just what he wishes for himself, is making the greatest of errors, for if he follows the lives of the great geniuses he will see that they have no time for anything except the time that belongs wholly to their Selves and also to the universe.

Let us consider this "free will" idea of the thoughtless. The God-Force of Natural Law says to us that man has free will to do just as he chooses, but God goes fifty-fifty with him on that idea and reserves the right to the *reactions* of all man's *actions*. So with free will, man may do as he chooses but he finds that the reactions to his actions are recorded very carefully in time and space. God looks out for that with Nature's electric-recording principle. Every thought and action is electrically recorded in space by wave forms. If these wave forms are unbalanced in their positive-negative, fifty-fifty divisions, Nature sees to it that they must eventually become balanced. The power of the whole universe insists upon that. From that law of balance there is no escape. None can avoid it.

There is also a record of all that happens *within* our bodies as there is in space, and also a record of the debit-balancing reaction to them in both body and space. If our action is a good action, the reaction is a good one and we feel no discomfort. We are not made to pay for it. If the action is unbalanced, we must pay for it as surely as the day follows the night even if it takes ten reincarnations to balance it. It is inevitable. We cannot escape it.

The universal law of balance is that principle of equal interchange between all creating things which preserves both the unity and the continuity of the universe.

Mind centers and controls body for the purpose of giving form to ideas through thought, and not for the purpose of indulging the body in unbalancing sensations.

I shall describe to you that thinking of the mystic by means of which you may rise from the position you are in to any other position you desire by understanding the relation of your body to Mind, and the principle by means of which Mind controls your body.

I shall read to you from *THE DIVINE ILIAD* concerning the creative purpose of thinking. This knowledge is vital to all who wish to achieve intellectual or economic supremacy.

"All thinking is universal thinking.

"All thinking beings are thinking in unison. All are creating that which they are thinking.

"All thinking beings are self-creating.

"All thinking beings are creating all things.

"Man is his own creator. Man is creator of all. This shall man know when he shall think within the higher octaves of Light of his Mind.

"When man shall know the language of the Universal One, of whom he is a part, then shall he know the voice of the Universal One speaking within him in the light of universal rhythms which man knows as 'inspiration.'

"What the Universal One is, I am. What He

146

commands, I command. My purpose is His purpose.

"God lives in me. My inheritance is from God and of God. He gives all to me. He withholds nothing.

"The divinity of me is Thine and mine. It is that which is recorded within the Soul of me. It is the Holy Spirit within the sanctuary of me.

"I am an idea of Thine. The body of me is the idea of the Soul of me. It is Thine and mine. I am the Master Sculptor. My body is the plastic clay. My Soul is the mother-mould of my body, the matrix for my regeneration.

"I am what I am. I shall be what I desire to be.

"What I am, I have desired to be. I am the sum of my own desire.

"I am Thou, Creator of All. Thou art I, Creator of All. I am Thou, Creator of myself, for Thou hast made it known in my heart that I am not of myself alone. I am Thou and Thou art I. I am of the far-thermost star and of the blade of grass in my door-yard. I am of my brother and of the mountain.

"The ecstasy of my thinking varies the spectra of ten times ten billion stars and illumines the ether of endless space.

"Thy thinking has created all that is. My thinking is Thy thinking. My thinking has created all that is.

"I am man, Self-creating.

"I am God, Creator of man.

"I am father of my Self.

"I am Son of the living God.

"The ends of space are mine. I shall know no limitations which are not Thy limitations."

This is the attitude of Mind in which the super-thinker should approach every big and little task.

The words, *"Ask and ye shall receive"* are just as true today as they were of old, but we must have a different comprehension than that of old, a comprehension which has been given to us because of our electric awareness. If we do ask with that knowledge, and act in accordance with Natural Law, we shall achieve anything we desire.

It is that idea of super-achievement which is so paramount in the International Business Machines Corporation. It permeates the entire organization from Mr. Watson to the office boy.

Supreme achievement and supreme belief in one's Self must be acquired by the same observance of Natural Law that liberates the artistic genius from the demands of his body when he feels some great inspiration flowing through him from the cosmos to which he must give form.

The genius approaches achievement with reverence. There is nothing in him of the wise-cracking youth who approaches everything superficially. No great work can be achieved in industry, economics, art or science which is not approached with reverence.

I will relate a personal experience of my own to illustrate this point. I had been a painter all my life and had never handled clay, but it became incumbent upon me to do a bas-relief of Thomas Edison, purely because of an accident. I was President of the Society of Arts and Sciences, and we were to give a medal to Edison, and the sculptor who was to have made it failed me. I wired Mrs. Edison that I would come and do it myself.

To do such a thing as that, which required a sudden change of medium from a familiar one to which the automatic reflexes of the body had been trained to an unfamiliar one which required new skills, is like a violinist suddenly changing his instrument to a piano.

It was very unwise for me to do this because with such a great man as Edison as my subject, I might not have survived had I failed. But my knowledge of my unity with the Universal One and the fact that I *must* do this thing, plus the inspired belief that I *should* do it as a demonstration of my unlimited power, made me ignore the difficulties.

So I went to Florida with a mass of clay, but on my way down I spent the entire time in meditation— connecting myself with the Universal Source—to realize the omnipotence of the Self within me, in preparing myself for what I would otherwise be unable to do. The result was one of the greatest mileposts in my career.

If I had followed the usual procedure of the superficially-minded man and played bridge all the way down instead of approaching this mountainous hurdle with reverence and insulation of Mind from body demands, I know I would have failed. In fact, I knew in advance, from long experience in trying to achieve the unachievable, that meditation and communion with God to gain greater comprehension was the only way to meet that challenge.

The communion which I have just described is the basis of the powerful creative thinking of all super-thinkers. It has no relation whatsoever to the sense reflexes of the body whose electric reactions we so often mistake for thinking.

All men who achieve epochal things in any walk of life live very serious lives and sound great mental depths. Dignity immunizes them from superficial thinking or acting and they accept the responsibilities of life with becoming gravity.

Extreme modesty characterizes the very great mental genius for he finds his glory in the humble service which is his to give to the unfolding of the divine plan.

All down through history, the leaders of men are inspired to achieve "impossibilities" against the resistance of those whose lack of vision limits them to their electric sensing which they mistake for thinking.

Their inspirations are always in the nature of an inspired "revelation," which we call a concept. It is always the "vision" of one who pictures in a flash something which may take years of time to unfold, but who can never be swerved from his belief in his ability to unfold the pattern of his vision after he has conceived it within him.

Consider Mr. Watson's vision of about thirty years ago. I know that he conceived this organization as a finished picture to which he must add one brush stroke at a time over many years to perfect. I know this, for I know the mental processes of the genius-mystic whose every thought and action of life must be in balance with the electric rhythm of the patterns which he has conceived—and from which he will not be swerved.

Consider Jeanne D'Arc as an outstanding example. She had a "vision" through which she saved France against overwhelming resistance. Her Consciousness could so insulate her from body sensing that she became wholly Mind. She exceeded the state which we call "genius" and arrived at that mental mountaintop of the great mystic, but there is nothing supernatural about that. When one transcends the body and becomes consciously aware of the Cosmos, one is then enabled to talk with God, for God and Self of man are One.

Her execution did not discount her achievement. For her death meant nothing, any more than it meant to Jesus. If she knew in advance that she would be burned at the stake, she would not have faltered for one moment. The mystic considers purpose alone, desiring only worthiness to fulfill it.

I can well conceive her exalted attitude of Spirit in her silent whisperings, during which she must have prayed within her Self somewhat as follows:

"Make Thou me a worthy messenger.

"Be Thou me. Thy power be my power. Thy essence my essence.

"Unfold Thou Thy concept through me.

"Be me that I may not be myself alone. Be me that I may be the universe.

"Speak Thou through me to all mankind.

"I am all mankind. Command Thou me."

To anyone who enters his day of achievement with that spirit, unlimited power is given. One who has that realization of omnipotence within him cannot possibly fail. Personally, I have learned to approach all my work in that spirit, whether it be the making of a monument or of sweeping my studio. Every task which must be performed should be made an art of, and executed joyfully.

Not all of the work of an artist is glorious. Much of it is drudgery. The true artist must love the drudgery as well as the glory, and this applies equally to the salesman, executive or housemaid. Each day when one crosses the threshold of his day, he must enter it with a feeling that he is but an interpreter of part of the divine plan.

I am not speaking to you in the religious sense nor am I preaching goodness or morality. I am telling you that in order for you to live and achieve anything of glory whatsoever, you must live according to Law, whether you know the Law or not. The Universal Law of Balance requires that each decision you make is one which does not hurt your body nor disturb your conscience by hurting others. If either one of those things happens, you cannot do good work. The body must be kept perfect and in balance, and it can remain in balance and in perfect health only if your thoughts and actions are in balance with the Universal Law of Love. Your body will be unbalanced and toxemic if your thinking is not true to your knowing.

You would not expect much of your radio if you abused it, nor can you expect much *conscious awareness* if you abuse your body. Your body is your receiver and transmitter. Through it you tune in to whatever rhythms you choose to take out of space, whether they be jazz or symphony. From it you also broadcast that which is your idea of your Self. People know you by the broadcast you give out from your sensed bodily machine. You, yourself, tell all the world whether you are jazz or symphony.

As a climax to these thoughts, it is well to point out the difference between creative thinking of the Mind and automatic sensing of the body. A great engineer might be heralded as a great genius for having created and built a great bridge. The bridge was the engineer's design, but practically all of the engineering principles that entered into that bridge were not his creations.

Like the building of man's body, it began ages ago and was added to gradually. All past engineering principles became a part of the electrically stored up memory records of his brain.

He performed a work of genius by knowingly assembling the elements from information gained in technical schools. His genius, as expressed by his bridge, was manifested by his cosmic power of inspiration to conceive idea and his knowledge of how to assemble the elements of idea into visual form.

Beethoven, for instance, assembled known elements into forms and rhythms of his own imaginings.

He was deeply inspired by that mood of Nature which imparted to him that certain rhythmic pattern of electric wave-form which always characterizes the light of the moon.

In that ecstatic frame of Mind, inspired by the rhythm of the night, he interpreted his concept into the form which we know as the "Moonlight Sonata."

One might claim that if Beethoven interpreted that concept from space, the "Moonlight Sonata" must have already existed and he *copied* or clairvoyantly picked it up. Whenever we create anything, we merely give form to an idea which exists in space as a wave rhythm. Creative thinking lies in the ability to conceive a rhythm and then give it a form which would cause others to feel the same emotion that the moonlight gave to Beethoven.

Fifty other musicians might have become inspired by the same rhythm and felt the same emotion sufficiently to have inspired them to write moonlight sonatas. If each one wrote his interpretation of that rhythm, all fifty themes would differ, but each one would give his hearers the same emotion. The extent to which man and God become One in their thinking is the measure of a man's genius or of his cosmic Consciousness.

The creation and the building of a spider's web is a wonderful feat of engineering. Yet the spider is not a genius because he built that web even though it demonstrates sound engineering principles.

The spider did not create that structure by thinking it out. At least not *that* spider. Billions of generations of spiders created that cobweb a little at a time by desiring a means of trapping food. The Creator thus gives to all creating things that which they desire for their survival.

Again we have the repetition of creative thought added to sensed matter in the nature of automatic reflexes. The spider's body is an electrically-sensed machine which turns out cobwebs just as any machine turns out the product it was designed to produce. Each part of the spider's body has been patterned to those certain electric rhythms of space which store up that idea of creation and preserve that idea through repetition. All ideas of creation are recorded in space for repetition as they unfold.

It is true that the spider directs his own body machine—but so does man. All bodies must be directed, controlled and motivated by Intelligence acting through the body by way of the senses. *Desire* is, however, the extent of the spider's thinking even though his product is the creation of genius.

The spider could no more help building that web than it could help breathing. The entire operation is automatic-motivation automatically responding to the hunger reflexes of his sensed body.

The beaver builds a wonderful dam. That is also a marvelous feat of engineering. The beaver dam was created in the same way. Through thousands and thousands of generations of building his body, plus the necessity for protecting his body, the beaver has evolved that dam a little at a time, generation after generation. The dam-building idea is a part of him. It is as much an extension of his brain as his legs and claws are extensions of his body.

If all the beavers of the whole colony were killed and one beaver alone survived, he would build the dam as perfectly as though a hundred beavers survived, and as naturally as the new-born calf would seek the proper place to have its first meal. Each merely obeys automatic reflexes instinctively. Instinct is not thought.

Very few people have as yet become thinking beings. Very few think at all. They merely act in accord with the demands of their senses and actually do very little original planning, assembling, designing or creating. *They imitate the thinking of others who do think.*

Are you willing to accept your present environment? Are you satisfied with your last achievement, your last picture, your sales quota for last month, or the speech you made last night? Of course you are not—nobody is. One should never be satisfied, for when that happens progress ceases, ego multiplies and one becomes static and stagnant. To express the God-force within us, there should be constant growth and new power with each moment.

To acquire new power, one must first seek the kingdom of heaven within himself. By so doing, Jesus said: ". . . *and all these things shall be added unto you.*"

To be in tune with the rhythms of the Universe is the secret of all man's power and greatness.

VIII

KNOWING VERSUS SENSING

I shall read to you from The Divine Iliad.

"See thou no more with outer eyes alone, for thou hast knowing eyes to void the illusions of thy sensing.

"Throughout long aeons man has walked his earth with eyes of outer seeing, giving belief to that earth of his body's sensing. Throughout his new aeons he must walk with eyes of inner seeing and know Me in it as but visioning it in Light of Me and Light of him.

"For I am a patient God. I patiently await awakening man.

"Awakening man is he who knows the Light of Me in him. Man may choose his own aeons for his awakening, but know Me he must. Until that day man's agony of unknowing shall be man's alone. His knowing must be his own desiring.

"Whyfore be thou slave to thy sensing. Rise thou above thy sensing. Be Me in thy knowing."

We live in two universes—the universe of sensing and the universe of knowing. The universe of sensing is the visible material electric universe of motion with which we are familiar. The universe of knowing is the invisible universe which we cannot sense. Man begins his existence upon this earth with sensing only. He has no knowledge whatsoever when he begins. He lives entirely in the instinctive electric universe of sensing.

The nerves of his body are what make him aware of his material existence. Sensation is what he feels with his body. He is electrically aware that he has a body. Electrical awareness of his body does not mean that he *knows* anything because of that awareness of his body.

Sensing and knowing have no relation to each other. Sensing consists of vibrating waves of two lights of matter in motion. Knowing consists of the One Light of Spirit which is still. The one still Light of knowing centers all motion, just as the still fulcrum centers the moving lever.

There is no motion in a fulcrum. All motion is in the moving lever which extends from the fulcrum. Likewise, there is no power in the moving lever which extends from the fulcrum. The power which is manifested by the lever is in the fulcrum upon which the lever oscillates.

Those who manifest God's knowing are moving levers which oscillate upon the still fulcrum of God's

One Light of *knowing*. They first manifest Him through the senses as motion. They then become Him through conscious knowing.

Civilization progresses in cycles of unfoldment just as all things in Nature unfold in measured cyclic periods. The cycle of transition of men from one stage to the next is nine years. Every nine years of man's journey through life and death, he becomes transformed. The desires of his childhood, boyhood, youth and manhood change as he acquires knowledge and experience because of having passed through those stages.

The cycle of transformation of mankind as a whole is approximately twenty-five hundred years. Civilization is forever in transit. Life is a journey from unawareness of any thing but body to full awareness of Mind in body. It is a journey from wholly sensing without knowing to wholly knowing without sensing. It is a long journey of many millions of years of just pure physical sensation of the body of man before spiritual Consciousness begins to dawn upon him.

Man has passed through those millions of years of jungle life of sensing and has recently emerged from that jungle into the dawn of conscious knowing. He has begun to know God in him, and for a few thousand of those many millions of years he has been searching for that God of which he has been vaguely "aware" through the hearing of inner whisperings within him—and through the teachings of messengers whom God sends periodically for the purpose of nurturing that growing awareness.

But our state of civilization is still very low. We are hardly far enough beyond the edge of the jungle to classify ourselves as other than barbarians. We surely cannot classify ourselves as God-like men while we still kill, rob and exploit other men and nations. Mankind as a whole is still in its barbaric stage but is making strides toward rising above it. This coming cycle will be one more step toward his omniscience.

We are deceiving ourselves into believing that we are a highly civilized and cultured people, possessed of great knowledge. Instead, we are in a period of transition in our unfoldment which is between the animal of the jungle and inspired man who knows God in him.

The fear of the jungle is still in man. He fears other nations of the world as tribes in the jungle fear other tribes. Nations maintain vast armies and navies for fear of other nations. We lock our doors and police our streets because of fear. The jungle man had no knowledge of good and evil. The jungle world killed for survival, for that was natural law. Man has begun to know the principle and necessity for unity, yet he still practices jungle methods in his human relations. He still believes that he must kill to settle his disputes with other men. He has not yet learned to "turn the other cheek."

In this present stage of seemingly high civilization, great nations are practicing this jungle principle of killing in building their empires with full knowledge of good and evil. Those who live by the sword will die by the sword for that which man sows he *must* reap.

Two thousand years ago, God sent messengers to give new comprehension to man. The idea of kindness and brotherly love was given to the primate world of that day, but man still refuses to practice it.

Our comprehension of natural forces has increased so phenomenally out of proportion to our spiritual advancement that we are in danger of complete destruction of the human race. We are using new discoveries and skills to multiply our ability to kill for greed and power. Man's desire for material advancement has so far exceeded his desire for spiritual advancement that the tremendous unbalance between the two will destroy both unless the desire for spiritual awareness overcomes the unbalance between the two desires.

During those aeons in which man knew nothing, living wholly as instinctively-controlled and electrically-sensed animals, he created absolutely nothing, just as animals create nothing. The apparent creations of animals, such as the spider's web or the nest of a bird, are created by the One Thinker, controlling His creations through instinct.

The moment man became aware of God in him, he began to *know*. With knowledge, he began to create. He became co-Creator with God, for there is but one Creator. That was the first step in his transition from sensing to knowing.

There was very little of *knowing* in that first step. In thus becoming aware of something higher in him, he began to observe effects with his senses, then to *think* of those effects, then to *reason* and form conclusions regarding what the evidence of his senses told him about those observed effects.

Out of these observations man developed skills. He reasoned how he might do things by combining the effects observed by him with other effects until his bodily skills in combining effects observed by his senses, supplemented by his thinking and reasoning, have brought him to this seemingly advanced stage of what he mistakenly thinks of as great knowledge.

Knowledge has played a very small part in giving the world of today the inventions and products of this electric universe such as radio, radar, and the chemical and metallurgical implements of our daily use, and the means of world transportation across seas of water and air. Knowledge cannot come through the senses. The senses of the body cannot know anything. Knowledge is spiritual. It is Cause. Man cannot know Cause by observing sensed effects of cause. He can but be informed of those effects and photograph their images upon his brain.

The brain of man is a part of his body. It is a mass of integrated electric waves in violent motion, centered by the still Light of Consciousness. Waves of motion cannot *know*—they can but feel. Our Consciousness alone knows, and man has been unaware of his Consciousness during all of these aeons of his jungle days. As yet he has but little knowledge and a vast amount of information.

His senses have given him a great electrical awareness of effects of motion but his just dawning Consciousness has, as yet, given him but little spiritual awareness.

Information gathered by the sensed eyes of the body by observation of matter in motion is known as empirical knowledge. Empirical knowledge acquired by the senses is subject to the countless illusions of motion which deceive the senses. For this reason, our so-called vast store of empirical knowledge is as unstable as the motion which caused it.

Knowledge is a spiritual quality. It has no relation

to the senses. The senses can observe and record, but they cannot *know*. They can be electrically aware of effect and can act through reasoning and thinking of the dawning conscious awareness of man.

Electric awareness is physical. It is the electric action of *thinking* one's *knowledge* into form—but *thinking* is not *knowing*.

Thinking and reasoning from observed effects of motion registered on the brain have given marvelous results in physical products but unless there is knowledge of *cause* back of the results, the products which man speaks of as his *creations* are but sense-observed effects *assembled* into form. They are not Mind creations born from spiritual knowing.

When a cosmically-inspired composer conceives a symphony, he is creating a product born of knowledge which he is thinking into form. His product is cosmic, for it comes from the Soul. But when a composer puts together many units of other musicians' creations, which he has become informed of through his senses, he is but assembling information into form. His product is physical because it comes from the body. It lacks the depth of a cosmic creation. The genius in it is not his own.

Another great illusion is that knowledge is written down in books and that we acquire knowledge from books. Knowledge cannot be written in books nor taught by teachers. Even the teachings of the world's great mystics, philosophers and geniuses are but information—electrically sensed by those who read or hear them until Consciousness of the Spirit recognizes them as knowledge.

The teacher cannot give knowledge except by reinspiring others with his inspiration. In order to do that, he must himself be inspired. Inspiration is the language of Light. It is the means of intercommunication between God and man. Written or spoken words or musical rhythms have no meaning for anyone unless the inspiration of knowledge in them is conveyed to him who reads or hears them.

Words or music are but information, or sound, electrically recorded upon the senses of man unless, and until, they become transformed into conscious knowing by reaching the Spirit. Man can repeat them just as a phonograph record can repeat things, but there is no Soul in music, no inspiration in words, unless there is knowledge in the performer or speaker which inspires him to reinspire his hearers.

The man who lives a sensed existence prefers a crowd. He never wishes to be alone. He never wishes to be silent or quiet. If he is in a room alone, he turns on the radio to make sound. If he is not satisfied with what he hears, he will turn the dial to something else, always something else—changing the dial—

changing the sound to make other kinds of sound. He will pick up a newspaper and read it while the sound is going on, not knowing the meaning of the sound—not even caring as long as his senses are being activated by it. He will read a story and not know what the story is telling him. If you ask him an hour later what he has read, he does not remember. He did not desire to remember. He cannot even tell you the plot of the story or the substance of the plot. He has forgotten it as he read it. The sound of the radio, the story, the plot, the advertisement, all are a jumble in his senses. They are all mixed together as he reads and listens simultaneously. In this manner, he spends his whole life entertaining his senses. If he goes out into Nature, he seeks a crowded beach, a boardwalk or dance hall—where the music is jazz. He sells a lot of goods—makes a lot of money— dresses well—and stands as a man in the community who is successful. You like him, and I like him. He is cheerful—he is a good fellow. He is well informed, but he knows practically nothing. His viewpoint is a materialistic one—he wants to be *shown*. His desire to make money and spend it exceeds all other desires. He is the dominant character in our industry and commerce. His name is legion.

On the other hand, the man who consciously lives

168

in the spiritual universe of knowing is as different as the obverse side of a medal from the reverse. Money is his last consideration.

From such men comes world culture—people who love to be alone and find ecstasy in it. It is from those who knowingly commune with God in Nature that the stupendous rhythms of our fine arts, our music, architecture, painting, sculpture, poetry and literature come. Without increasing world culture, our civilization would retrogress.

What would our world be without the enriching influence of the great masters who have given us our priceless works of art? Think what it would mean to take great masters of music out of our lives, such as Wagner or Rachmaninoff. When we contemplate such a catastrophe to our mental enrichment, we can better realize the inestimable value which just one such genius living knowingly with God is as compared with one who lives a mere sensed existence.

Yet it is through these geniuses who live in the world of knowing that those who live in the world of sensing ascend to the heights. That transition from the material world of sensing to the spiritual world of knowing is continually taking place among men. The more one listens to the rhythms of heaven, the more one becomes attuned to them. The lover of jazz to whom a symphony would be painful gradually reverses his desire as he re-attunes himself to spiritual rhythms.

Likewise, his sense of beauty undergoes the same transition, and with it a love of Nature.

All men are seeking to become higher beings. It is innate in all men.

The great desire for that higher understanding which can alone come from God is permeating all the peoples of the earth at this period of chaos in world affairs.

This is the new dawning day of the greatest spiritual awakening in all man's history. New comprehension will give him a new sense of values—a new understanding of his place among men—of his relationship to the universe, and of other men's relationship to him.

Man must comprehend and obey the Universal Law of Love and thus manifest his inheritance of omniscience, omnipotence and omnipresence.

IX

THE SECRET OF CREATIVE
EXPRESSION

In the heart of each and every one of us lies buried
the seed of creative expression, *but the awareness of
it is what makes some geniuses or mystics,* while others never rise to great heights. No one need be des-
tined to oblivion. We are all born with exactly the
same inheritance from our Father. All that God has
to give, He gives to everyone alike. The only difference between one man and another lies in the measure of his awareness of his relation to God, and the
knowledge with which to become co-Creator with
God.

There is but one Creator in the universe,—one
Mind, one Person, one Being. We are that Creator,
that Person, that Being in the measure that we *know*
we are.

We must know the universe and its underlying
principle for only through knowing, through having
a scientific foundation under our knowing and an
awareness of God dynamically—not abstractly—can
we become creators.

Following is an extract from The Divine Iliad which is The Word of God—an inspired message given to man, which I have interpreted for man's understanding.

"I am the Knower of the Known.

"I am the sexless Knower of the Known. In Me is the Consciousness of all-knowing. And that is My power.

"In Me, the unconditioned One, is the Whole. There are no parts, nor are there beginnings, nor endings in Me, the One Conscious Whole.

"I am the dual Thinker of unfolding parts of the Known, the Imaginer of imaged forms which emerge from My knowing, through My thinking, to manifest My knowing.

"My dual thinking divides My knowing Light into pairs of sex-divided mirrors of the two opposed lights of My thinking. These electric mirrors of divided light reflect My Light and Life in them for manifesting My knowing and the One Life of My Being. Forever and forever they interchange the dual reflected lights of My thinking for manifesting the continuance of My thinking, yet they are not My Light, nor are they My Life.

"Nor are they My Being. I, My all-conscious Being, alone live. And I alone think.

172

"Again I say, all thinking is My thinking. Also I say, when man thinks at all he thinks with Me as One, imagines with Me as One, and builds his images with Me as One.

"And when man is inspired by exalted thinking know thou that it is I in him who am thinking as One within him.

"For I am the Source of ecstasy and inspiration in man. Behold in Me the Silent Voice which man may hear who hath inner ears to hear. And I am the Light which man may see who hath eyes of the Spirit to see.

"For I say that in-so-far as man knows the ecstasy of inspiration in him he hears My Voice and sees My Light in him. He then knows the mighty rhythms of My balanced thinking and thinks with Me."

That is the keynote—the very crux of power in man—the KNOWING of the Creator within him; hearing His mighty rhythms and being in tune with those rhythms, with the vibrations of the light-waves of God's thinking from which he is extended and which he manifests by his thinking.

Be not forgetful of those underlying principles— of the fact that there is a fulcrum under every lever or wave of motion, and that man cannot get along without that fulcrum. A mechanic who desires to lift a ten-ton rock with a crowbar can do so only by putting it upon a still fulcrum. The power is in the still fulcrum and not in the moving lever nor in the expression of power extended from the fulcrum. God sayeth: *"Seek Me, know Me, be Me—be the fulcrum of thine own power."*

Desire is the very basis of Creation. God desires. Without His desire to express His knowing, there would be no universe of matter and space. Without desire in man, there would be no form, no product, no separation of idea into its many parts. God's idea is to divide the formlessness of His One Whole Idea of Creation, to take it apart for multiplication into many forms. Thinking does that. We think our knowing into many parts, then set those parts into motion to express the balance and the power of the centering fulcrum of the One still Light from which each wave of us is extended.

Now what we do with those extending waves of our thinking is what we make of ourselves. We can be what we desire to be. We are the product of our own thinking, but our thinking is what our knowing is. We *think* idea but we do not *create* idea. We produce something but that product of idea is not the idea itself. It is but the bodily form of the idea. The idea still remains in the formless Light of God, in the inspired Mind of the creative thinker who manifests God. Man creates nothing but form and motion to simulate the idea which never leaves Mind, never is separated from Mind. *Idea is cosmic. It cannot become matter, but it can assume material form to simulate the cosmic idea.* A watch manifests the idea of time, but it is not time. It is a product that simulates that idea, but it is not the idea. It also manifests mechanical principles, but the mechanical principles are not there. The wheels and other parts of the watch simulating that idea are there, but the idea is not. I, as a sculptor, produce a monument. The idea of the monument never leaves my Mind. The plaster, clay, or bronze forms and symbols manifest the idea of that product but they are not the idea which they simulate.

An ignorant man can see those same forms as well as I, but they mean nothing to him. Another Mind can be reinspired by it and reflect the inspiration which is in my Mind. My Mind is an extension of the Mind of God, for there is but one Universal Mind. In that sense, my monument is not my creation alone. I am but an interpreter of the Creator—a co-Creator with God. The entire material universe is but a manifestation of God's divine Idea. The Idea itself is within the One Light and never becomes a part of the two lights of motion which electrically record the Idea in form of matter.

Yet we continue to create product in a material

universe which is just a complexity of light-waves of matter and has no meaning whatsoever as idea. Then we wonder why there is so much mediocrity in the world. Product without knowledge and inspiration behind it can never become an enduring masterpiece.

It is as though a mechanic tried to lift a ten-ton rock with no fulcrum under his crowbar—or like science trying to do marvelous things with its levers of motion, denying the Spirit as its fulcrum of knowledge. Science studies effect rather than cause. It can prove effect of motion and matter but it cannot prove the cause of effect in the laboratory, so it relegates cause to metaphysics. Until science takes God in as co-Creator, it will never know the cause of the many complex effects. But science must know the cause. Science is at the crossroads where it must include the spiritual Source of its material effects.

Religion is at the crossroads also. Religion and science are as two opposites, but in the voidance of their opposition, unity will come to both—science the creator, religion the creator. They will have new knowing, new comprehension; disunity will become unity. A marriage between science and religion will remake our civilization.

There are millions of people concentrating upon producing product in matter, when the secret of creation is not in effects of matter but in the cause of those effects. For that reason we must reverse our creative process from product to the Source of the product. To do that, we must have knowledge. We must know the WHY of things. One cannot produce anything whatsoever in excess of one's knowing. One cannot be an interpreter of anything which he, himself, is not. To interpret God's idea, one must be that which he interprets. To the extent that he knows God in him, he is God. Knowing God, he can act the part to the extent of his knowledge. The greater the actor, the greater his ability to become the character he simulates. The greater the character, the greater the art produced by him.

So *be* that which you are creating. One cannot produce enduring things unless one has that knowing and that awareness of Being in Him from which his source of inspiration comes. There is but one Creator, one Thinker, one Being, in the universe. The nearer you come to becoming that One, the greater your ability to create, and the more enduring your creation will become.

Consider the musician who thinks only of his skill and technique in playing the piano. His product may be harmonious and rhythmic sound, but it is not art. Sound, even though rhythmic, does not reinspire or uplift another to the great heights of creative genius. To leave God out of any creative expression is like

digging an empty well. To take God in is like producing an ever-flowing well. The power of the Creator whom one is interpreting comes from the Soul.
Without that, music is nothing. Without that spark
of creative genius which comes from the Soul of a
sculptor, his monument would be nothing but bronze
or stone.

Likewise, the products of shops or factories would
be nothing but forms and bodies of matter. Civilization is living too much in the body—too much in the
flesh. It is not trying to give creative expression to its
ideas with a fulcrum of spiritual power under it.

Civilization is an instrument in the hands of the
Creator, working instinctively as animals work instinctively toward the one purpose of seeking for
something for their bodies. Man is doing the same
thing, also, to too great an extent—seeking for something for his body.

There is a power within the body—a power that
you and I can have for the asking—for the desiring;
and we must learn to use that power to upbuild ourselves. That is the thing we must do instead of just
building the body alone. Before we build any product, we must build our inner Selves up to the level of
the product. We must desire to produce. No man can
produce anything greater than he, himself, is.

Beethoven's "Moonlight Sonata" is his product

printed on paper. It can be played by a musician who is sufficiently inspired to reflect that great interpretation of a mood, but unless he has the Soul of a Beethoven he can never reproduce that Sonata as Beethoven produced it.

The greatest of sculptor geniuses, like Praxiteles and Michelangelo, and the great masters in music, could not have created their masterpieces unless they, themselves, were superior to that which they produced. We have very few geniuses, but countless technically-skilled parrot minds who repeat what they are taught without knowing in their Souls what they repeat.

What are skills? What do they mean? They do not mean Mind. They come by work. Anyone can develop a skill to play a musical instrument, to paint, to draw or to sculpture. There can never be a greater painting than the painter of it, however, nor can there ever be a greater product than the thinker of that product. Skilled people who lack Soul are mere automatons like machines, or like animals which display marvelous skills. Spiders are skilled automatic machines. They create marvelous webs instinctively, but have no more knowledge of what they are creating than an adding machine knows what it is doing. Countless skills are known in the animal kingdom, but there is no genius in the animals which manifest those skills. The genius of their creation is God, their Creator.

The beaver builds a dam. He builds it because he has built it for countless centuries, and he continues to build it instinctively and automatically, becoming a part of Creation—not co-Creator with God but an automatic extension of God's thinking, expressing God's idea in form, purely as an automaton. The idea of that dam is a part of the whole idea of Creation, extended through the Creator and through His Creation. It automatically takes place as a part of the work of the Creator Himself, supplemented only by the desire of the beaver to have that means of protection and food. The spider has the desire for something to catch flies and that desire is answered by the Creator.

Man has gone beyond that point, beyond that state of instinctive control. He has begun to think, and every thinker thinks with God because there is only One Thinker. If a man thinks at all, he is thinking with his Creator. If he creates, he is creating with his Creator. If he knows, it is because of the one Light of the Creator which is within him. Whatever knowledge he has is measured by his awareness of God within him.

I shall give you a rule by means of which you can check your relation to the two universes in which you live. You can gain much by applying this rule to every act. We live in two universes—the universe of *sensing* and the universe of *knowing*. The universe of *sensing* is effect of cause. The universe of *knowing* is cause. We cannot *know* anything that we can see or feel or touch. Things which our senses respond to, we cannot *know*. They are effects. You cannot *know* a sunset sky because it is a fleeting effect. But you can comprehend it because you know its cause.

On the other hand, you cannot sense that which you cannot see. You can *know* that which you cannot see, but you cannot sense it. I can sense the fact that there are many people here. I can see your bodies, but I cannot see you—the Person who centers those bodies. I can know you, and I can know you as a Being, but I cannot sense you. So we can sense God's body, which is His universe, and thus be electrically aware of it, but we cannot *know* the universe of motion. We can, however, *know* God, the Creator of it.

I know the head of a great industry. I knew him as an office boy who studied shorthand at nights to equip himself for a better position. He soon became secretary to the president, and finally vice-president of one of the greatest industries in the country. One day I asked him the secret of his success. He answered: "I have always wanted to be the man higher up, and I have always prepared myself to be the man higher up. I found that I could always become that man for there is more room at the top but very little room for the multitude who crowd the bottom. I am still equipping myself for the man higher up, for I find that the top of the ladder of success reaches into the high heavens, which is still far to go."

It is not intended that any man remain where he is when he starts his career. He must always progress to the last days of his life, but he can progress only by continually becoming a greater person, one having more comprehension, more awareness of the Light, more power to create his productions by being greater than that which he produces.

The secret of all success lies in building ourselves. Never mind the product, never mind the skills. They will come if we spend all our energies in building ourselves. Each of us must learn to be the fulcrum of his own power by becoming more aware of the Light that comes to us gradually during the long journey from sensation to Consciousness, and from mediocrity to masterfulness. The only possible way to acquire power is to recognize it in one's Self.

The kingdom of God is in every man. Seek it always. Let that search be one's only purpose in life. When one does find it, all things else will be added unto him.

X

SECRET OF MAN'S POWER

I shall read four excerpts from *THE DIVINE ILIAD* as my text for tonight's talk on the subject of man's Source of power.

"When they shall know the Light of Me in them, then they shall be Me and I them.

"When man knows Light, then he will know no limitations, but man must know the Light for himself and none there can be who can make words of it, for Light knows Light and there need be no words.

"Wherefore, I say to thee, exalt thou thyself beyond thy sensing. Know Me as fulcrum of thy thinking. Be Me as deep well of thy knowing.

"Until then he is but moving clay, manifesting not Me in him while sensing naught but moving clay of him; knowing not MY Light in him."

Every man wants to be great and powerful. The most important thing for any man to know who wishes to express power is his own relationship to the universe. Until he does know this relationship, he is like a blind weakling seeking his own way through the dark. His power is measured by the extent to which he knows his relationship to his universe. It is also limited to that measure.

Man's supreme error lies in thinking of himself as an individual unit of Creation. Practically the whole mass of mankind believes that each man is a power unto himself, independent of anything else in the universe. Each believes himself to be an individual entity whose thinking is his own, confined within his own brain, and who has power of his own within himself to act.

Very few think of themselves as utterly helpless in themselves. Very few know that they are as dependent upon their Creator for even the slightest of their actions as an electric light bulb is upon the generator from which it extends. The relationship between the electric light bulb and its generator—from which it draws its power—is exactly the same as the relationship between man and God—man's only Source of power.

An electrician is thoroughly aware of the fact that he cannot get any light whatsoever if he disconnects his bulb from its generator. To give light, it must be connected. To get more powerful lights from his generator, he must *know* how to make each individual bulb stronger and more powerful. It is only through such knowledge that the electrical engineer can multiply the power of a small candlepower light to the candlepower of a search light.

Likewise, the only way a man can multiply his own power from mediocrity to genius is to become thoroughly aware of the one supreme universal fact that GOD ALONE IS—and that nothing is existent but God. He who knows this knows that he of himself is nothing, but is all-powerful because of the Father abiding in him. Any man who knows the Source of his existence without reservation as to his own independent existence is already omnipotent, omniscient and omnipresent. The illumined ones alone have this knowledge in its fullness.

Only such men can say with full cognizance of its meaning, "*I can of mine own self do nothing. The Father within me doeth the work.*" Jesus alone, of all men ever born on earth, could say this with as full a certainty of its meaning as the electrical engineer could say: "These bulbs have no light in them. They can do nothing of themselves. Whatever light comes from them is extended to them from their source. It is not their own light; it is that which is in their generator."

Jesus knew God as the One fulcrum of the entire wave universe. He knew the nothingness, the unreal-ity of this Mind-imagined thought universe which only *seems* to be.

Jesus knew the orderliness of law and the processes of Creation; in fact, He was the world's only consummate scientist. Because of His scientific knowledge, He was fully aware of all creating things as being extensions of each other—all being one—all being the imaginings of Mind under control of Mind.

It was this knowledge which gave Him the power to heal and to perform the so-called miracles attributed to Him. Jesus was, therefore, the greatest man who ever lived because He had greater knowledge than any man who ever lived. Knowledge is the key that unlocks man's door to cosmic power. The more any man *knows*, the more powerful he is or can become.

Many of us try to emulate the example of Jesus with the idea of goodness in mind. Goodness or virtue alone will not make any man great, God-like or powerful. Goodness in any individual is the result of action according to God's law. Man must *know* God's law of love within his heart and Soul before he can live love. Emulation or imitation alone cannot make a man great.

A man must know within himself the nature of God and God's processes of Creation. When we speak of brotherly love, we must know its scientific meaning in respect to the unity of the entire physical body of Creation as well as the unity of the spiritual universe of God.

Jesus lived the principle of brotherly love with scientific knowledge of the unity of man. He knew the Oneness of the omniscient Light from which all things are extended to manifest the love principle of unity. He knew, also, the unity of the electric-wave universe of seeming many parts—and the balanced interchange of giving and regiving which manifests the love principle in matter. To Him there were no other men on earth than His Self—that all seemingly separate other men were His own Self—His own body—all being extensions of Himself as His arms were extensions of His body. He had not even the concept of separateness, for He knew the WHOLENESS of God and His One Idea.

His very idea of the brotherhood of man had no connotation of multiplicity in it. To Him brotherhood of man meant wholeness of man as ONE. When he said: *"Love thy brother as thyself,"* and *"Love thine enemies,"* He did not think of the words "brother" and "enemies" as being other persons. He could not, for the Oneness of the Father was in Him. Plurality simply did not exist in His Consciousness. The sum total of Jesus's knowledge transcended matter. To Him, man's material body was unreal, his Spirit alone being real, while to unillumined humans, man's body is real, being presumably controlled by Spirit.

Jesus was all that God is. He was the Light of God's all-knowing. Because of that fact, Jesus could knowingly say: *"I and my Father are One."* How few there have ever been who could say that knowingly. Perhaps none other than Jesus. We teach the Oneness of God and man in principle, and we include it in all of our religious and metaphysical literature as fundamentals, but who among men can divorce matter, multiplicity of mankind and the ego of individuality from his concepts of unity?

Man is sense bound. Only the greatest geniuses can transcend the senses and forget the body for a sufficient length of time to become aware of God in them for the purpose of interpreting God's mighty rhythms. Jesus was never for one moment unaware of God in Him as One. He forever transcended the senses of his electric body. He was wholly Mind, wholly omniscient, omnipotent and omnipresent.

God is Love—*unexpressed.* God's Creation is Love—*expressed.*

God's Love is changeless unity. God's Creation is His imagined division of His unity into pairs of changing opposite units, multiplied to infinity, for the purpose of manifesting the power of love through interchange between opposite pairs.

Love is the one supreme Whole Idea of God.

Desire to express love is the supreme power of God.

Knowledge of how to express the power of love makes any man who has that knowledge supreme over other men.

The *divinity* of any man is the measure of the Light of Love in him.

The *power* of any man is the measure of desire to express his divinity.

The *greatness* of any man is the measure of his ability to express love in his human relations in the manner in which God expresses love in Nature.

God is balance. God expresses His power in Nature by balancing His opposed pairs. Creation consists of two unbalanced electrical conditions which forever seek balance in each other to manifest the unconditioned unity of balance from which they extend as moving waves.

God expresses His Whole One Idea of love in Nature, electrically, by *rhythmic balanced interchange* of love between all pairs of electric opposites in His imagined universe of multiple units of His One Idea. *Rhythmic balanced interchange* between pairs of opposite conditions is God's one law by means of which all effects in Nature, or in man's world of human relations, are produced. God holds this one law inviolate in all effects of cause.

God always balances all of His effects of interchange in His creating universe. Man persistently unbalances so many of his effects of interchange with other men that balance is impossible for him. All man's ills, his failures, enmities, worries, fears, diseases, and wars are the result of breaking that inviolate law. The extent to which man breaks God's law is the measure in which he, himself, is broken.

Civilization is a gradual unfolding of the comprehension of the nature of God and the processes of Nature working out its complexities of effects under the one law of love.

Civilization progresses in the measure of that comprehension exemplified in its great men. Its great men are those who know God in them and interpret His rhythms in accord with law. Its great men are always few. Those few constantly uplift other men by a constant raising of the standards of world culture.

When there are too few men living knowingly with God, civilization becomes decadent. The world is in one of its decadent periods now because of that fact. Material-minded men have conceived greatness to lie in the expression of physical and mental power

over other men, and in the material power of possessions.

Mankind has not been demonstrating the principle
of love for his fellow man. Men and nations have
sought to enrich themselves with material possessions
in utter defiance of the law of love. Men whom the
world has considered great have been God-less men
who ruled kingdoms with iron hands, and gathered
together large amounts of gold and other material
possessions. Others whom we have considered great
were those who delved into the secrets of chemistry
and electricity to produce the material for enriching
empire builders of industry for self-enrichment.

Greatness in man has been associated with money
and material power. Many there have been of this
kind whose names are forgotten in a few generations,
but few there have been of such immortals as Wagner, Beethoven, Rachmaninoff, Shakespeare, Socrates, Leonardo or Michelangelo. These are the men
who uplift the whole human race because they work
knowingly with God, while those who work for self
alone pull the standard of civilization down to lower
levels.

This generation is not producing such spiritually
great men as even two generations ago—such men as
Longfellow, Whittier, Milton, Emerson, Scott,

Dickens, Blake, Tennyson, and Poe. Even the last generation produced such musicians, poets, writers, painters and sculptors as Victor Herbert, Sibelius, Rachmaninoff, Elizabeth and Robert Browning, Walt Whitman, Mark Twain, Kipling, Markham, Masefield, Augustus Saint-Gaudens, Daniel French, Frederick MacMonnies, George Gray Barnard, Burne-Jones, Keats, Whistler, Inness, John Sargent, Monet, and hosts of other geniuses in the arts, here and abroad.

When so many geniuses lived contemporarily, world culture arose to high points to direct man's thinking into spiritual channels. Where are their equal today? We are not producing them!

All of our arts are decadent. Ugliness has taken the place of beauty. In painting and sculpture, the ugliness of unwholesome thinking and practicing has flooded the land with the distorted works of men whose personal appearance and manner of living are as decadent as are their works. Beauty and dignity can come only from creators whose inspired lives are dominated by love of beauty. This generation can count all too few such men. Those who have set high standards for past salons have died. The salons which they made into temples of beauty are fast becoming tombs for art's decadence.

In no department of life has decadence of morality been felt more keenly than in religion. The reason for this deplorable condition is because dogmatic and creedal religions have outgrown their usefulness in this electric age of greater comprehension.

The old hell-fire and brimstone of orthodoxy no longer frightens people into being good. Orthodoxy, such as it was, held people to a greater practice of religious devotion than it possibly could in these more enlightened days. The God of love is replacing the God of fear in man's concepts. Fifty years ago, practically the entire population went to church, and the child who did not attend Sunday school was rare.

Today, sixty million people in this country do not regularly attend any church, and a very large percentage of children do not attend Sunday school. That does not mean that people are less desirous of religion. It means that creeds and doctrines which have been inherited from pagan days are no longer applicable to this more enlightened generation. Sin has a different connotation in this electric age.

People no longer can be convinced that the naturalness of birth is sinful.

Because of the many beliefs of early day religious teachings, over a hundred different disunited creedal religions sprang into being. The world is on its way to finding unity. A disunited church can never unify mankind.

A church which depicts the nature of God as any other than love cannot exist. The god of anger who must be appeased by sacrifice for the remission of man's sins appeals to the ignorant but not to the intellectual.

The comprehension of man has risen far above man's willingness to accept such concepts.

We have come to the eleventh hour in our civilization where God's Law of Love must rule *all* mankind. We must have One World with One Religion of Love.

Until the Law is lived by all men, we shall continue to produce materialistic men who destroy world unity. We are at a crucial point where the whole world *must* produce great men who know God in them—men who manifest the love principle upon which the universe is founded—or perish. The world concepts of values in human relations must change from accent upon money and material possessions, which are transient, to accent upon spiritual values which are eternal.

The material-minded man who seeks gold can obtain more gold by working with the law of love than without it. *This he does not know.* New comprehension, born of the spiritual awakening arising from new-age teaching, will gradually transform man's concepts of power and greatness. The principles of human relations must be reversed from the practice of *taking* for material self-enrichment to the practice of *giving* for mutual enrichment. He who thus acquires treasures of earth will simultaneously acquire treasures of heaven.

The dread serpent of fear of our neighbors which forces us to lock doors, police streets and arm nation against nation, will disappear only through the complete reversal of human relationship practices to conform to Nature's law of love. When one obeys the law and gives of himself to his fullest extent, the law will unfailingly work to regive in equal measure that which he has given. Nature unfailingly observes this law in both action and reaction. Rains from the heavens given to earth for its needs are regiven to the heavens by unfolding forests and other growths which the heavens need to produce new moisture.

Consider how the law of *rhythmic balanced interchange* would work in industry. A shoe manufacturer, for instance, considering his own interests, restricts the credit of a customer who is in financial difficulty. Practice of the love principle by the manufacturer would be demonstrated by him in sending his efficiency expert to consult with his customer and help him find a way to overcome his trouble. The expert may find him carrying too high priced shoes for that neighborhood and advise a sale of different grade shoes made suitable for his neighborhood needs.

Instead of losing a customer by assisting in crushing him, the manufacturer would have continued to keep a customer by solving his financial problems through extension of the love principle. In addition to the values in money received by the manufacturer, he has the loyal friendship of the man to whom he has extended love. This is the priceless asset which does not go down on the books of earth but is unfailingly written upon the records of each man's soul for eternal repetition.

When man adds the priceless love asset to each of his dealings with other men, he will be adding universal power unto himself which continues to repeat itself automatically as his heart continues to beat, or as the rains continue to regive to earth for earth's givings.

This love principle is slowly being applied in industry. Even where it is applied only in part, or as good policy, it is giving wonderful returns in the dollars which may still be the motive back of the practice. The practice of *rhythmic balanced interchange* as a policy alone will unquestionably bring back more dollars—but dollars are all it will bring. The treasures of heaven can never be acquired by one who seeks the treasures of earth only by using the cloak of heaven.

Ethics alone or goodness alone, no matter what the services of man for man are for which ethics and goodness are applied, will not constitute greatness in a man or in an industry. Higher wages, or even profit sharing, are often voted merely as good policy for making more money. These principles bring more money, for they are for the betterment of man and must, under the law, bring returns in kind—but the returns are only in kind—and no more—for if love alone is not the motive, love will not be returned in addition to dollars.

The workings of universal law in respect to such transactions are clearly set forth in *THE DIVINE ILIAD*, in Chapter VI, verses 8 to 13, in *Book of Desire*, as follows:

8. *"Verily I say, he who giveth in My name, storeth up great riches in the rhythms of heaven which are as immortal as the Soul-seed of his Self is immortal.*

9. *"But he who taketh riches in his own name, giving naught of his Self to Me to void the greed of his self-taking, gathers naught to himself but riches which are as mortal as the clay of his earth-self is mortal.*

10. *"Things alone of earth which man desires are but things of earth to be returned to earth with bones of him. But things of earth, heaven blessed by Me, are as eternal in the immortality of his Self recording Soul as Light of Me is eternal.*

11. *"He who desireth riches of earth alone, denying Me in him, shall dwell in outer darkness of his own making until he shall desire Me strongly.*

12. *"E'en to him will I give all he asketh without stinting, yea, and even more; but he, having more than all he sought will have naught but worthless dross of his earth desire.*

13. *"And darkness will enshroud him. No Light will there be in his eyes, nor will he know Love. Having desired the dark without My Light, he will have but acquired the dark."*

The ideal of the new age is one world—one people. It will be many generations before that ideal can seem to have the possibility of consummation. The race is still too new. We are still in our barbarian state of taking by the power of might-over-right. Democracy is not two hundred years old. Freedom is but a concept in the throes of expression. Rulers of empires owned their people, to exploit them as they willed—even to kill them as they willed.

Races and languages are too many and too separative. Such a condition assures disunity. In the millenia to come, there will be but one race and one language upon the face of the earth, and the beginnings of that have been assured and precipitated by the shrinkage of distances which have made the whole world next door neighbors.

One world can only come through strong men throughout the world demonstrating the love principle by living it and teaching it. We are not producing strong righteous men in our governmental bodies. When the fires of freedom burned strongly, we bred statesmen to whom patriotism, freedom and love of country were more than their lives. Men like Washington, Franklin, Jefferson, Paine and Lincoln are not being produced in these decadent days. Such men governed people *for* the people. Instead of such righteous and patriotic statesmen, we are producing such men as Hitler, Mussolini and Franco who use their offices for the expression of personal power. Politics has taken the place of statesmanship and patriotism. Moral and ethical decadence in world government is as marked as it is in the fine arts.

It should be the supreme desire of governments, heads of industry and education, as well as of parents, to produce great men, great patriots, statesmen, philosophers, musical, artistic, literary and scientific geniuses, to stem the tide of moral and mental disintegration which is lowering world culture. Only a renaissance of human genius will lift the standards of civilization to higher moral, mental, and spiritual standards.

Edward Markham says: *"In vain we build the city if we do not also build the man."*

Civilization must obey the law of love in order to endure. It must find balance and the knowledge necessary to retain balance. It might be well to review man's life purposes and desires in simple postulates and axioms for the purpose of building a concept of a balanced civilization.

FIRST POSTULATE

Man lives in two universes; the physical universe of *sensing*, as manifested by his body and body needs, and the spiritual universe of *knowing*, as manifested by his desire to seek inspiration from the Light within himself for the purpose of becoming co-Creator with God.

AXIOM

Man and God are One. To the extent in which man knows God in him, he is God and has His omnipotent power.

SECOND POSTULATE

Man lives on two planes—the idealistic or intellectual plane of concept, and the physical plane of the materialization of his concept.

200

AXIOM

In order to create, man must have inspired knowledge of cause from God and information concerning effect of cause from man. A balanced education should be one in which knowledge of cause and information concerning effect are equal.

THIRD POSTULATE

Man's whole life is spent in thinking his knowledge into form through action, and resting in order to repeat his thinking and acting.

AXIOM

The standard of civilization is the sum total of every man's knowing, thinking and acting.

FOURTH POSTULATE

Man and his environment are the product of his thinking. They are what he made them. Their forms are the images of his conceptions. Conceptions are spiritual. They are cosmic. Conceptions of idea are never produced. Forms of product are physical. Physical forms of spiritual idea are alone produced.

AXIOM

Cosmic man is transcendent. The product of inspired cosmic man is alone enduring. The product of physical man is transient.

FIFTH POSTULATE

Man desires the omnipotent power of intellectual

supremacy and the use of that power in creating himself and his environment.

AXIOM

Man's desire to create can be fulfilled only through the power of knowledge extended to man by God. Man has no other power. He who desires to create enduring things must knowingly work with God.

SIXTH POSTULATE

Man seeks two kinds of possessions; physical possessions which he creates from materials borrowed from the earth for the use of his body—which must be returned to earth with his body—and spiritual possessions which are eternal and cumulative during his entire unfoldment.

AXIOM

The measure of a man's greatness is the measure of his knowledge and practice of God's law of love— of his good or bad judgment in relation to his thinking and his acting, and of the balance he sustains while acquiring his physical and mental possessions.

SEVENTH POSTULATE

Culture is the measure of man's spiritual and intellectual status, and his environment is the measure of his culture. Culture is the basis of all courtesy, manners, consideration for others, good taste, civility, poise, emotional control, and all personal expressions in ethics and human relations.

AXIOM

A progressive civilization is one in which the qual-
ities of civil human relations are in the ascendant.
Prosperity, happiness and peace are dependent upon
civil ascendancy, spiritual and intellectual advance-
ment and cultural growth.

EIGHTH POSTULATE

Man's measure of culture, prosperity, happiness
and peace is registered in his environment. Environment is the material evidence of a standard or
ideal. A village, town, city or nation reflects its ideals
in its environment.

AXIOM

The material of environment is the only product
of industry.

NINTH POSTULATE

Ideals are born of inspiration. Ideals reflect the
divinity within us. The higher the ideal, the higher
the standards of civilization. The higher the standards of civilization, the more beautiful the environment.

AXIOM

Beauty is the symbol of love, balance, truth, and
the orderliness of law. Beauty is the keynote from
which the octaves of the symphony of Creation are
extended in interchanging Light of God's thinking
as expression of His knowing.

203

TENTH POSTULATE

Beauty is the only product of the arts. Science is the catalyst which binds art to industry. Religion is the science of spiritual expression in human relations.

CONCLUSION

A perfect civilization is one in which art, science, religion and industry are equalized as the result of balanced thought and action.

PART III

QUESTIONS ANSWERED

GOD IS THE ONE STILL LIGHT.
CREATION IS AN EXTENSION-
RETRACTION OF STILLNESS
INTO SIMULATED MOTION.

I

QUESTIONS ANSWERED

Q. *Why is it you are able to answer all of our questions upon any subject so easily?*

A. Because all knowledge exists and one can have all knowledge by desiring to have it. To quote from *THE DIVINE ILIAD: "All questions are answerable in Light. Thou art Light. Thou can'st answer them."* You can answer them as well as I if your desire for knowledge is sufficiently intense.

Let me call to your attention, however, that I cannot answer questions which are not knowledge. I could not tell you the date of Julius Caesar's birth, for that is not knowledge; that is but information. Knowledge is limited to cause. Information concerns effect. Effect belongs to the sensed electric universe of motion. Motion cannot be known. It can but be comprehended.

$$* \qquad * \qquad *$$

Q. *What is the underlying principle of motion?*

A. The universe of motion is founded upon a very simple principle, as simple as your heartbeat or your incoming-outgoing breath. All effects are the result of the two desires of the Creator for expression of His idea. One desire is for division of oneness of idea into multiple forms of ideas. The other is for a return to oneness for repetition of multiplicity through rest. Each of these desires is expressed by half a cycle of two-way motion between two opposite points of rest to other opposite points. Each opposite voids its other opposite, but our senses do not detect this fact. If they did, they would sense the illusion which the universe of motion is.

All effects of motion are the result of either balanced or unbalanced interchange between the pairs of opposites which manifest God's two desires while on their respective journeys to and from the rest points in the Light from which each is extended.

* * *

Q. *Have you any simple key, or formula, which helps you answer questions?*

A. Yes. My knowledge of the wave is the key.

* * *

Q. *Tell us about the wave.*

A. The wave is the foundation of God's creative expression. By means of light-waves God expresses His two desires. There can be nothing more simple than the wave principle of equal giving and regiving for the purpose of repeating the giving and regiving. Complexity lies only in multiplying simplicity. The principle that two times two are four is simple, but the same simple principle applies when you multiply 5648 by 4872. All you have done is to create the idea of complexity by multiplying simplicity. That in no wise alters the simple principle.

When you learn to think in terms of the wave, you will find yourself living in another world. The more you know the light-wave which records God's thinking, the more you will be enabled to think with Him. The more you think *with* God, the more you will know, for God is all knowledge and His knowing will be your knowing.

*　　*　　*

Q. *What is meant by being One with God?*

A. The more you are aware that the Light of God centers you, the more you become aware that that Light is your very Self, and that your body is but an extension of your Self which you have created to manifest your Self.

The more that awareness grows, the more you become the cosmic Being and the more you know. When you finally become fully aware of that Supreme Being as your very Self, you ARE that Supreme Being.

*　　*　　*

Q. *Why can we never see God but can know Him?*

209

A. Over and over again I say, you cannot know that which you can see. Remember that. Also, anything you know, you cannot see.

Just as you can see man's body but cannot see man, you can see God's body but cannot see God. Conversely, you know man and God but cannot see man or God. Furthermore, you cannot know man nor God, nor your Self, until you know the Light which you and man and God ARE.

*　　*　　*

Q. *What do you mean by God's body? Has God a body? If so, what kind of a body—and how can we see it?*

A. The universe is God's body which He created by extending His Light of His Self to manifest Him, just as man extended his body from his Light to manifest man.

The whole universe is an electric light-wave record of God's desire to create form to manifest His idea. Likewise man's body is an electric light-wave record of man's desire to create form to manifest the man-idea.

I can see your bodies because your bodies are the recorded effect of your creative thinking, but I cannot know your bodies. The Person of man, or the Person of God, is invisible. The Personal Being cannot be seen but can be known as the CAUSE of His own EFFECT, extended from Him as body. Again I say, you cannot know anything which you can see or feel, or cannot see or feel that which you know.

*   *   *

Q. *Do you advise against reading, studying, and our modern education?*

A. I certainly do not. The reason this question was asked is because I happened not to have been brought up that way. All my life I have known God in me, and when I wanted knowledge I was immediately aware that I had it. God had given it to me as He gives it to all people. So God became my teacher. For that reason I had no need for books or schools or universities.

My education was cosmically acquired because I knew God in me. Knowledge can be acquired cosmically if one *really* knows God in one instead of abstractly *believing* it without *knowing* it. It is really easier to acquire it by the hard effort of sensing it through the physical body.

*   *   *

Q. *How could you know such things as chemistry that way. Did you not have to study books to make your chemistry charts?*

A. I could not have made my chemistry charts if I had studied books or taken a university course. No books or universities had that knowledge, for it had not yet come into the world. Also I would have been bound by the traditions of yesterday's errors of thinking by accepting them as truths, as most students do when they read the works of "authorities" and listen to older teachers to whom they attribute great knowledge.

* * *

Q. *How can a person acquire a cosmic education? How can he KNOW things just out of the blue?*

A. It is not "just out of the blue" as you say. You, of course, mean the invisible universe. All knowledge is of the invisible universe. That is what I mean by the universe of knowing.

We are all being educated cosmically to some extent, whether we know it or not. Our inspirations come that way. Our inspirations are God's whisperings to us in His universal language of Light. If desire for knowledge is in our hearts or we write that desire upon our hearts, we will have that knowledge just as sure as the sun goes down over the horizon at night. We are getting it that way gradually during our whole journey from the jungle to the mountain top. If the Light comes slowly, it is because the desire is weak and belief too vague and abstract.

Education is not just stamping upon your memory all of the things that you have read in books. If that is all that happens, you have been made into automatons that are little better than machines. You would repeat records that phonographs can repeat in the same way. If you study music that way and are only a technician, there is no music in you, there is nothing of the spiritual in your knowing.

But if you have taken the skill and information that you have acquired in school from your teachers and you have let it sink into your very Soul, then you have art in you. You have then made the great transition from sensing to knowing which makes geniuses out of those who would otherwise be mechanicians.

*   *   *

Q. *You said that when you desired knowledge, you were immediately aware that you had it. Does God give knowledge that way—instantly?*

A. Yes, but not as you understand it by the way you stated it. We *have* all knowledge in us. It centers us. It is our inheritance. The Light of our Selves IS all knowledge. We become aware of it gradually as we desire it. We recollect it as we desire it.

Just as the whole of the tree is in its seed before it unfolds, so is the whole of man in man's seed. Likewise, all knowledge is in the Light which centers man. It unfolds as man desires its unfoldment.

We are all being cosmically educated to the extent that we so desire to be thus educated. The trouble is that mankind has not yet become sufficiently aware of his oneness with God. He is not willing to believe that he can actually commune with God as Self and

Self. He thinks of God as outside of himself, as a Deity so superior to himself and so outside of himself that he believes direct contact is impossible.

*   *   *

Q. *You actually believe we can contact God directly?*

A. Most assuredly I do. How can you reconcile the teachings of universal oneness in the Light to any belief of separateness, or the "crawling worm" and "miserable sinner" attitude of those who cannot think of God as a moment-to-moment companion?

*   *   *

Q. *Is that what you mean by a cosmic education— that you are actually taught what you know directly by our heavenly Father?*

A. Most assuredly, yes. You ask that as though you think it strange! Why should the unity between the Creator and His Creation be strange? The moment you actually KNOW of your oneness with your Father in heaven, you KNOW that the kingdom of heaven is within you.

*   *   *

Q. *What relation should our school education be to our cosmic education?*

A. Your school and university education must be the foundation or basis of your cosmic education. When you read a book for an hour, ask yourself about it for another hour. Think it over. Ask it of your Inner Self. Something in you will tell you whether it is truth. Knowing-Mind does not register untruth. It registers only truth. Whatever you read that is not in accord with Natural Law will eliminate itself. You will not be able to recognize it as truth so your Consciousness will refuse to accept it.

A school education is necessary for cultural reasons. I do not decry it. I say you must have it, but I had to go faster. I had to demonstrate power for the purposes of giving this Message of The Divine Iliad to the world, to accelerate the spiritual awakening which is now taking place, and for laying new foundations for religion and science.

* * *

Q. *How can we apply our school and university training to our cosmic training?*

A. By developing your creative faculties as you acquire encyclopedic information. Demonstrate in practice what you learn from books and teachers. Memories stored upon the brain are electrically alive. They are like little entities which want to be heard by being repeated. Make use of them.

* * *

Q. *My boy, in college, has the ambition and the determination to become a great orchestra leader. What preparation would you advise?*

A. To be a conductor, one should be a performer, but not necessarily, for a great conductor can concentrate his attention purely upon the knowledge of music and can then conduct. No man can give more than he has in him, however. No one can manifest that which is greater than himself. A flashlight cannot give the light of a searchlight. A conductor, to be a great conductor and give of his fullness, should also be a good performer. He should learn to perform as well as to conduct, just as the great preacher or teacher should be able to manifest that which he teaches by being able to do it.

The preparation for the conductor is to begin to study music itself and to perform on any instrument—a dozen instruments if possible. Perhaps Walter Damrosch is as great a conductor as we have had in this century and he was a marvelous pianist. And, on the other hand, there are men like Gabrilowitsch who was a great pianist and also a great conductor. He did not practice conducting so much as he did playing, but he could do each equally well. He conducted an orchestra in Detroit and he went about the country playing as a concert pianist.

* * *

Q. *You knew Gabrilowitsch, did you not? Will you tell us something about your association with him?*

A. Yes. I knew him very well. He was a musician all the way through.

It might interest you to know that when Gabrilowitsch posed for the bust I did of him, he looked no more like a musician than a colonel in the Army, or a lawyer. After half an hour of work, I said, "I want to see you as a musician. I want to see music in your eyes. I want to see the very soul of music in you because that is what you are. I do not want to do a bust of you just as an ordinary human being." "What shall I do?" he asked. "Go to the piano and play," I said. "I cannot play for an audience of one. I could play for an audience of a thousand, but not for one," he replied. "Yes, you can," I replied, "you just play and forget me and I will take care of my part." He played for an hour or two at a time for sixteen hours. I was then able to interpret him as a musician. I think that is one of the best things I have ever done—it portrays a man actually inspired by thinking music.

*   *   *

Q. *I feel that I have been called to write. Can you give any help or suggestions about my preparation? Where shall I go to study?*

A. If you want to write, start writing. Whatever you want to do, start doing that thing now, this very minute, not the next minute. Before you start studying anything, start doing that thing first. You will then find out what your faults are.

217

Try to write something. Then go and ask a master what is wrong with it. Show him what you have done. He will know the struggle that you have gone through and will point out your faults. You will know what he means because of your efforts. But if you have done nothing, you have not made any faults to point out.

The person whose desire is keen in him to do something, and starts doing that thing—learning how to do it in the doing of it—will be the one who will become a master, and no other.

* * *

Q. *I know that the wonderful freedom of easy breathing, just as the keenness of the senses, is closely associated with inner-feeling. Is there any simple rule that might be applied to bring about that condition of ecstasy which is characteristic of cosmic conscious people or even to induce meditation?*

A. There is no necessity for a technique or formula for meditation. Inner-feeling, or inner-knowing, is the Silent Voice of inspiration within us. One automatically breathes easier as desire for effort ceases. The more forgetful one is of one's body, the more one is freed for the transition from outer emotions to conscious stillness.

If one desires that ecstasy of being in the God-Light, breathing will become effortless. It will slow the heartbeat also by relaxing the body. One of the greatest means of relaxing the body is to stop thinking and meditate—to become one with the Spirit. That is the reward of living the conscious life—the most wonderful thing that can happen to anyone.

* * *

Q. *How can sounds affect the heartbeat?*

A. If a woman sings a lullaby to her baby, its heartbeat slows down to the tempo of the lullaby and the body relaxes. Various sounds, like the honking of horns—the noise of a boiler factory—the turning of a radio dial from one tempo to another—are all conducive to physical sensations which increase the heartbeat.

The quiet of the mountains, forests and calm sea are conducive to the slowing of the heartbeat. They free the Mind from body-sensing in order that the Silent Voice of consciousness can be heard.

* * *

Q. *Did Jesus know all things? I mean by that, did He have omniscience?*

A. Yes, He did have omniscience. He was undoubtedly the only man who had known complete Cosmic Consciousness.

* * *

Q. *Can a cosmic conscious man see Jesus as a person?*

A. No one has ever seen the Person of Jesus—or Beethoven—or you. The body alone can be *seen* and the Person alone can be *known*.

* * *

Q. *Are Jesus and God the same?*

A. Yes, they are One—and so are you One with God when you *know* that you are.

* * *

Q. *What is the Soul?*

A. Soul is the desire force in Mind, the *will* to extend desire from the Light to manifest the Light in form.

* * *

Q. *How does desire manifest itself?*

A. Without desire, the seed would not germinate into form. The Soul centers the seed in the pattern of desire to express form. The seed records the pattern of the body as it changes throughout eternity. The record changes according to the desire of the Soul-will to become a different body.

* * *

Q. *Could you give an example?*

A. Yes. The pattern of a tree in Maine where the winds blow hard is recorded in the seed of that tree. The same ruggedness of pattern will be recorded in the seed and repeated as the same kind of tree when the seed again unfolds.

Q. *Your statement that trees have Souls as well as human beings is rather extraordinary. Would you explain it further?*

A. The Soul is universal in all things. It does not belong to man alone. God is Light. The Soul is DESIRE in the Light. It might also be termed the WILL.

*　　*　　*

Q. *How does animal life differ from vegetable and mineral life?*

A. What you call animal life is not rooted to earth. It has entirely different bodies which must interchange in order to continue. The vegetable kingdom is rooted to earth. The mineral kingdom is the earth itself.

All of these function alike. They all begin and end in the same way.

*　　*　　*

Q. *What are their relations to each other? Which comes first?*

A. The mineral kingdom comes first—the planet is all mineral until sufficiently cooled by the coming of water. Interchange between water and minerals begets the vegetable kingdom.

Interchange between the vegetable and mineral kingdoms begets the animal kingdom.

Each of these three depends upon each other for survival. Each is an extension of the other.

II

QUESTIONS ANSWERED

Q. *"He who killeth an ox is as he who killeth a man."* (*Isa.* 66:3) *We are told that we have dominion over everything—does that mean we are to slaughter animals for food?*

A. In Genesis it was said that man shall have dominion over all things. Moses meant by that that jungle-man knew nothing of God. When he first became aware of God within him, he searched for his God in the sun, in the avalanche, or in anything that he could not understand, and built gods to worship. Moses wrote: "Let us make man in our own image, and let him have dominion over the fish of the sea, etc.," which meant that he had begun to KNOW instead of to sense.

Man never had dominion over anything until he began to know God in him. Then he began to create with God. He created the wheel; he discovered how to make a boat and then make a sail for his boat. He began then to have dominion over other things in the universe, which he did not have before. Knowledge gave him this power. That did not mean that

222

he was newly made—as Adam—in a minute. It simply meant God had been whispering to him for millions of years but he had not heard until that time. When he did have dominion, it was only because he became aware of God within him. When that unfoldment came, he then knew good from evil.

When he killed, as in the little fable about Adam, he knew for the first time that he was killing. The Garden of Eden was a symbolic contrast to the jungle. In the eyes of the future, he looked up to the mountain of his ascension and he began his *knowing* of good from evil. By killing, he knew that he should not kill. But we have not yet progressed very far from that jungle; we are still barbarians. Only two thousand years ago, they killed and slaughtered animals on the very altars of the churches to appease God. The altars of the churches in Jesus' time ran with blood because blood was the jungle memory of man and it still is. We fill our hymnals with songs about blood—blood of the lamb—fountains filled with blood—all sorts of things which indicate that we are still remembering the jungle.

We are not yet out of the jungle in respect to even our food.

* * *

Q. *What is your position on metaphysical healing?*

223

A. Everyone should know the principles of healing within himself, but if he does not know, anyone who does know can extend these principles to another and help him to heal himself. He can help with or without the other's knowing. We are all connected by invisible electric threads of light; these threads are cables by which we intercommunicate with one another.

*   *   *

Q. *Then you think anyone can help another by just desiring to do so?*

A. Yes! He who reverses that process and tries to make the circuit run the other way by taking all in for himself and giving out nothing gets nothing back but the toxins he, himself, has generated. Many are self-poisoned with such toxins, and all the instruction or friendliness of anyone in the world will not get rid of these toxins unless the individual cooperates by living and thinking according to the law. One can take in the good that is extended by the friend and give it back as good. He to whom unkind thoughts are extended must insulate himself against them lest he be injured by them.

*   *   *

Q. *How does one insulate oneself from such influences?*

A. By giving out love. Love alone insulates one

224

from hatreds and fears. You have heard it said that boys fall into bad company and thus "go bad." One does not need to do this; one does it from choice. If one yields to another's influence, he does it because he lowers the standard of his desires. This is a matter of his own choosing. He who loves can insulate himself from evil thinking by not accepting evil as a part of him.

* * *

Q. *How about a person slandering another or getting angry with him?*

A. The same question holds true. Ignore it and continue to love. Slander or anger will not hurt you unless you reflect it. If you become angry, you are hurt for you are no longer loving. If you ignore it, the slanderer or angry one alone is hurt because anyone whose thinking is opposed to love is hurt by the toxins which hate engenders to poison one's body.

* * *

Q. *What would you do if a beggar asked you for food?*

A. If I were convinced that he was sincere, I would give him food. I would try to discriminate, however, so as not to encourage vagrancy.

* * *

Q. *Will you tell us about telepathy?*

A. Telepathy is best understood by comparing it

with the cable. Telepathy is rapidly coming into conscious use as we get farther out of the jungle and nearer the mountain top. People send messages across a cable. We get another's meaning telepathically by a glance or a look without needing a visible cable. People separated thousands of miles think messages to each other through invisible cables of light.

Our spiritual unfoldment will one day make the use of telephone wires for sound transmission obsolete, for we shall then transmit our messages telepathically. We are, in truth, complete transmitting and receiving sets within ourselves.

*   *   *

Q. *Is not that what you mean when you talk about the language of light?*

A. Yes it is! The language of light is the Silent Voice of omnipresent *knowing* interpreted into lightwaves of universal *thinking*. Telepathy, inspiration and intuition come to us across the invisible lightwaves of the universe. They are our universal cables by means of which Mind speaks to Mind.

There is but one Mind and one Thinker. Therefore that which is *known* or *thought* by anyone, anywhere, can be known or thought by any other one who is sufficiently attuned to receive telepathic messages sent in the language of light.

Q. *Is that the way telepathy applies to man?*

A. Everyone and everything in the universe is connected by electric nerves which act as telephone wires to inform everything in the universe of the conditions and desires of every other thing. People who love each other very much, or who have a great mutual understanding, can use these inter-communication nerves to communicate with each other over long distances. Jesus understood thoroughly that when He walked *among* people He was walking *through* people. The electric extensions which bind all men together as one were clearly known to Him.

* * *

Q. *Please amplify your explanation. Tell us more about the idea of things happening within ourselves instead of outside of ourselves.*

A. It is very difficult for the objectively-trained brain to realize that *all things and all happenings are universal.*

We think that thoughts, sounds, and other happenings of which we become cognizant take place in other objects and in other places outside of ourselves. This objectivity of belief is not true to Nature. Everything which happens anywhere, happens everywhere.

There are not two points, two positions, or two

objects in the entire universe. Therefore, whatever you think of as happening outside of yourself is actually echoing within yourself.

There is no other place in the universe than that place which you universally occupy. Likewise, there is no knowledge or thought in the universe that is not omnipresent in the Light of you. The reflection of a light in a mirror is actually within the mirror. All Creation is a mirror which reflects itself within itself universally.

*   *   *

Q. *Is that true of our emotions concerning other people? If I love a girl, for instance, is she not another object outside of myself whom I love?*

A. No. You do not love another object or person outside of yourself. Your love is within yourself. She inspires within you the love which is within you. She has merely awakened within you something you have not, until now, been aware of. Love is not objective. It exists omnipresently.

The principle of this philosophy is beautifully explained in an essay on Love in the New Translation of Laotzu's Tao by Dwight Goddard. I would urge you to read it.

III

QUESTIONS ANSWERED

Q. *What is truth?*

A. I could answer that very simply, but it would be meaningless. Truth in its ultimate is rest—balance. God, the one Light, is balance. In Him is all truth. Many different words are used to define the nature of God, but they all have one meaning. We say truth, love, balance, the law, life—and the meaning of all of these words is the same in God. So when we say, "What is truth?" it is the same thing as saying. "What is power, knowledge, life and law?"

* * *

Q. *What is life?*

A. We think of life as a pulsation, a heartbeat, a thing that is living when its heart is beating. The body manifests life; it is expressing life; but the expression of life, such as a lever working upon its fulcrum, is not the life which is expressed. It is the lever, but life and power are in the still fulcrum— not in that which moves—not in that which pulses. Our bodies do not live; they but express the life of our Source.

Q. *What is thinking?*

A. People do not think in themselves; they manifest the knowing of God through a cosmic thinking which arises from their cosmic Consciousness. People do not think with their brains, for the brain is but a storehouse of memories and a center of nerve ganglions which motivate the body. Consciousness is universal. It is not confined within anyone's skull. The brain acts as Consciousness directs. It acts to manifest the *thought* of God through the *knowing* of God.

* * *

Q. *Although I have a quick, bright mind to catch on to things, I am always slow to get things from the ether. Sometimes several days will elapse between events that I finally figure out but do not get at the moment. I am always behind time in everything I try to do, no matter what effort I put forth. Why?*

A. You are trying to *think* it out instead of KNOW it. There is no power at all in thinking unless there is knowledge behind the thinking. One must have a concept of an idea before one can take that concept and express it. You are like the child that the teacher tells to concentrate on some subject and write an essay. You cannot concentrate until you decentrate and get the knowledge to concentrate upon. Decentration is for the wave motion of thinking to expand into cosmic Mind stillness. First, get that knowledge by desiring it; then bring it to a focus; then write it down to give it form.

Stop thinking, be still; be alone—meditate. You know what you want to know. You have a desire to know something. Write that desire into the stillness of the Light within you, which is God within you, and give God a chance to answer you. Do not stifle His Voice. Wait for it, listen, and it will come, just as a theme for a beautiful symphony will come to the musician who desires it.

* * *

Q. *When you know the Light and receive the flashes of guidance, in attempting to follow closely, how can insurmountable obstructions in the physical be handled? There are none in God, yet they stand in the way of expression.*

A. There are no insurmountable obstacles on earth anywhere. In any undertaking, whatsoever, hurdles are put there to be surmounted. The hurdles that cannot be surmounted are self-made. Their limitations are set by man himself. God does not set them.

* * *

Q. *Is it necessary to take vitamin pills and capsules for health?*

A. It would not be necessary to take capsules and vitamin pills if we had a properly balanced diet of natural food, such as fresh vegetables, fruit and nuts.

However, our present mode of living, and the way we cook our food, often creates a deficiency of necessary vitamins. Scientific research has already produced gratifying results in capturing valuable vitamins, thus supplementing deficiencies.

* * *

Q. *What causes goitre?*

A. The lack of iodine. I traveled through a whole section of country when I was sketching in Switzerland in which many people had very large goitres because the glacier water they drank was deficient in iodine. Vitamin pills containing iodine, or a few drops of iodine in the water, is remedying this trouble. One sees very few goitres there now.

* * *

Q. *Then you do advise supplementing food with vitamins?*

A. Yes! Always supplement if science can give you what you cannot otherwise get in food. Your body is a chemical plant and it needs certain replacements for deficiencies made by its not being possible to get them in the diet. People in cities live rather artificial lives and we must meet that problem by artifice to keep our balance.

* * *

Q. *How can one accomplish more work without tiring?*

A. The person who gets tired is the one who does not like the work he is doing, or who has over-taxed his body-machine by giving it more work than its normalcy. If one is bored by one's work—whether that work is making beds, washing dishes, mowing the lawn, or anything else which one dislikes doing— toxins are developing which make one tired. The clock-watcher in the factory gets tired, but the man in the laboratory or in the factory who is wishing that the clock would stop because he has not sufficient time to finish what he is doing loves his work and does not tire.

* * *

Q. *Please expand the idea of loving to do such drudgery as washing dishes and making beds?*

A. A lady wrote me once that she hated making beds and washing dishes. I said: "Whenever you find that you do not like what you are doing, just remember that God centers you, and whatever you are doing you are doing with Him and with His help. You cannot move your little finger otherwise. When you make your bed, just say, "Come, God, make this bed with me."

Later she wrote: "That made me love to make beds and do things I did not like to do. Knowing that God was helping me took away that feeling of loneliness and drudgery."

Take joy in doing things; find happiness in doing everything the best way you can. If you have to do it, you must do it, so you might just as well love doing it. If you really love your work, you will not tire. Conversely, if you hate your work, you will poison yourself by that hatred and the poisons must be removed by an understanding of the universal law of balance. Any other form of relief which does not remove the cause can only be temporary.

*   *   *

Q. *Does the genius get tired?*

A. When I was sculpturing Thomas Edison—and he was in his eighties—he said that he never tired because he had so much to do. When he was through with a day's work, he would start something else. In the morning when someone thought he ought to rest, he might say, "Come down the road with me, will you? I want to find some weeds." He was experimenting to find rubber at that time. Although he was always doing something, he never tired. He did not know fatigue because he loved his work.

You never knew a musician who was writing a symphony to be tired; or a sculptor to be fatigued when he was creating a monument—something they loved to do. You never knew a boy to be tired when he was playing a game he loved; he might get sleepy—but never tired. You could pick him up and carry him home when his legs would no longer carry him, but he loved his playing. One can become sleepy because the body must rest, but one who gets tired does so simply because he does not like what he is doing.

Love what you are doing and you will never know fatigue.

* * *

Q. *I am a very enthusiastic golfer—shoot around eighty as a rule. I love the game but find the last few years that eighteen holes tire me exceedingly. What is the cause?*

A. You cannot expect your body machine to function as well at seventy as it did at forty. I would not expect one to play eighteen holes at eighty. I painted a portrait of Bishop Alexander Garrett of Texas once. He was eighty-two, and all the time I was painting him he was telling me all the things he was going to do. His mind was young and full of ambition, but his body was not able to carry out those things. His desire and ambition caused other people to carry them out for him. In this manner, he achieved his desires by extending those desires to others so they became physically manifested through them.

I should think that you would be quite content with playing nine holes at your age. I am quite content with two or three hours of skating now, where I used to do ten and even more; for I am seventy-six, and two or three hours is enough.

But to come back to golf: this man who wants to play eighteen holes at his age could play the eighteen holes if his desire were strong enough. God fulfills reasonable desires. By "reasonable" I mean lawful. Nature fits the back to the burden. Desire is the foundation of all achievement. I know a man of eighty-three who walks fifteen miles every Saturday.

*   *   *

Q. *Will you expand this idea a little more by giving examples?*

A. The Consciousness makes the body obey. The body is electric. Electricity is the servant of the Mind. Electricity will do what Mind tells it to do and it will make the body do things that it could not otherwise do. Supposing you wanted to lift a heavy trunk suddenly. You know it is heavy—you know you have to move it—to lift it up. Make up your Mind that you have to do it and electric action will shoot adrenalin from certain glands throughout your body to make it possible. The glands of your body will give the power that was not there two minutes ago, and you will *know* that you *can* move the trunk.

Everyone has done things like that under the spur of the moment when the desire was there and it was necessary to do so. People often refer to that as using superhuman strength. It is not superhuman; it is normal, but you asked for an increase of strength and your desire was fulfilled.

You then realize that you have power you have never used. We never use the full limit of our power, but desire for power gives us power. If it is essential that you play eighteen or more holes of golf in a day, and you want to do it, you can still do it even if you are ninety. One of the members of our New York Skating Club is eighty-three and he still skates wonderfully well.

* * *

Q. *Is it true that in the final analysis there are only two opposites; and if so, what are their names?*

A. Yes, there are only two opposites. God has divided everything into two opposites—two opposite halves of a cycle. One half of every cycle expands; the other half contracts. Every cycle is a journey from rest to rest by way of contraction—or expansion. Rain falling on the earth manifests compression. Mist rising from the earth expands to complete the cycle. Rain generates—mist radiates.

All opposites are, in every case, extensions of a centering equilibrium. The equilibrium which centers

237

them is their source from which two opposites are extended, as the lever is extended from its fulcrum.

* * *

Q. *Could you give us some examples?*

A. Yes! Compression and expansion are represented by matter and space, by the earth and the heavens; by positive and negative, by the male father principle and the female mother principle. Compression and expansion are also manifested in the mechanical principle of a piston in an engine which moves to express power. But the expression of the power is not in the compression or in the expansion. The power itself is in the still center which lies between the two. The dead center is the fulcrum upon which each wave-lever moves to express power. It is the one balanced condition.

In an electric battery, we have two opposite conditions which we call negative and positive. They are the two opposite extensions from the fulcrum—like children on a seesaw—from which the piston of motion operates. An electric current interchanges between these two opposite electric pressures. But the power is not in the electric current; it is in that dead-center between them across which they oscillate. That equilibrium is their source. All the current of electricity is gradually voided in the dead-center source of rest from which it came.

If you want to recharge a battery, you must borrow the two opposed conditions from its dead-center. Two opposed positive and negative conditions must be created from the one balanced condition so that the two unbalanced conditions can interchange to manifest the One universal balance from which they sprang.

If you put a short wire across two unbalanced opposed poles and short circuit them, they go back to a balanced position of rest immediately. Or if you put a little wire across, you may light a hundred electric light bulbs for a day or two while the electric current slowly goes back to its dead storage battery condition of rest. The effect is the same as though a short circuit did it in one second.

*   *   *

Q. *Can you give an example in time concerning that effect?*

A. Yes! If an explosion takes place in a second, it fills a tremendous volume of space. A seed from an oak tree expanding slowing for a hundred years fills an equal volume of space. One we call an explosion and the other we call growth but the principle is the same. Each is an electric interchange between two opposite conditions of dense matter and tenuous space—of earth and the heavens—of seed and the tree. The interchange between the slow growing of

239

a tree from its seed is exactly the same as the interchange between matter and space in an instantaneous
chemical explosion except in point of time.

* * *

Q. *Is all Creation made up of opposites?*

A. Yes! All Creation is made up of pairs of opposites, and all opposites are two opposite electrical
pressure conditions. Each opposed pressure is extended from the One Light which centers it. Also,
each pressure is either plus or minus its centering
condition. All we have to deal with in this universe
is the One Light of the Creator and the two lights
extending from the Creator which manifest His
knowing by His thinking. This universe is an electric
record in black and white light. The white light of
suns is the pressure of compression, and the black
light of space is the pressure of expansion. Each interchanges constantly. The out-breathing and in-
breathing of all bodies manifest this constant interchange between matter and space. This interchanging
process constitutes the universal sex principle.

* * *

Q. *When complete rhythmic balanced interchange
has been attained by the individual, will not that
eliminate the cycles of birth and death?*

A. Yes! The continual rebirth and death of an
individual named Johnny Smith ceases when the cos-

mic awareness of his identity and unity with God is complete. That is what the whole play is for. It is the journey from sensation to conscious awareness of God in us. But rebirth and death will continue through age-long cycles in newly polarizing bodies to repeat the same process of unfoldment from individuality to unity.

This process fulfills the universal principle of Nature, which is that individuality springs from Oneness and returns to Oneness. It is inevitable because the universe consists entirely of waves of motion which spring from stillness and return to stillness.

* * *

Q. *What about reincarnation after we have found completion in cosmic conscious awareness of unity with God?*

A. When that time comes, the planet will be way out where Mars is—or beyond—and Venus will be rolling up getting ready to play the man-idea all over again.

The planet is entirely mineral until water appears upon its surface. Mineral is the first kingdom. Mineral and water then interchange to unfold vegetable life—the second kingdom.

Mineral and vegetable then interchange with water to produce animal life—the third kingdom.

Mineral, vegetable and animal life then interchange with water to unfold physical man—the fourth kingdom.

Unfolding from man of the fourth kingdom comes cosmic man of the fifth kingdom. The play is then finished on Earth to be played over again on Venus.

IV

QUESTIONS ANSWERED

Q. *Could you tell us more of the restoration of balance in the eternal whole, and how this marvel comes to be?*

A. It is not a question of restoration of balance in the eternal whole. Balance always IS. Restoration only *seems*, for unbalance is but an illusion of motion. Two children on a seesaw get out of balance, but the unbalance is always balanced in the fulcrum. The fulcrum is always in balance with the universe. This explains the reason why we cannot sin against God or His universe. We are extensions of God. He is our fulcrum. Whatever "sins" we commit are but unbalanced effects of motion which are balanced in our universal fulcrum.

In other words, if there is disunity in your family, business relationships, or an upset state of health, this indicates unbalance. To bring harmony, successful business, or perfect health and happiness, one must find the cause of the disunity and ill health, etc.

Financial lack is often the cause of disunity in the home, and also of ill health. Disunity in the home, poor business and ill health may all spring from the same cause—unbalanced business conditions which have been created through unfair exchange in either labor or goods.

Man does not yet realize that that which affects him *personally*, affects all other men. He has yet to learn that he is not a law unto himself.

One unfair business deal can not only affect his business life, but his home life, his health and family's health, and many others who are closely connected with him.

When man is happy, he is balanced. When he is unhappy—whatever the cause—he has created unbalance. We hear men say repeatedly, "How can God allow such things?" The reason for this is that God is always in balance but He gave man free will to express himself. Man by his own actions creates his own unbalance and, therefore, his own unhappy conditions.

* * *

Q. *Does this mean that all our ills, failures and unhappiness, and even war, are brought about by ourselves?*

A. Most certainly, yes. God does not prevent man from working out his own destiny. That is what the whole play of life is for. If God prevented man from hurting himself, man would not progress through experience. However, by so hurting himself, he cannot in any way hurt or offend the Creator who remains forever man's fulcrum—man's God of love.

*   *   *

Q. *How can one develop balanced rhythmic breathing?*

A. One's normal breathing is balanced and rhythmic. We are all born that way. One can increase the power of that breathing if one desires to by giving more power to one's muscles, tendons and sinews, by exercise and deep breathing. One can add power, perhaps, but that is merely a multiplication in a higher key of rhythmic balanced breathing. The electrical engineer steps up his electric potential by multiplying the coils of his solenoids. This multiplication divides their diameter and thus increases wave frequencies in the coils.

*   *   *

Q. *Wouldn't a person progress faster spiritually if he could leave his daily round of chores and lead a more solitary life for at least a little while—in the mountains or woods, or by the seashore?*

A. Yes! If it is possible, one should do that; and one can also learn to lead a solitary life in the midst of even boiler factories and noises. In the daily round of chores, no matter if it takes the whole of one's waking hours, one can learn to lead the solitary inspirational life. One has a right to be alone with God. Cultivate the ability to lead an inspired life under all conditions.

*   *   *

Q. *Do all geniuses go alone into silent places to create?*

A. No! One of my greatest musical friends tells me that some of his deepest inspirations come to him while riding in subways. Think of it—being inspired in the noise and clutter of subways. My answer to that is that he needs the stimulus of motion rather than solitude to inspire him. Many do seek the woods, seashore or forests. I like to be alone in my studio. When alone, I have the seashore, woods, and all else that imagination and inspiration bring me.

*   *   *

Q. *Can you completely forget the body when alone?*

A. One can only forget the body and become acquainted with oneself by being alone. There is no condition whatsoever that shuts man out from that possibility. Cease thinking—cease acting with the body—be utterly alone and comfortable. That is the way to forget the body. That is why so much comes to one in the night. One can then forget the body— put it on the shelf so to speak—and be entirely alone with the conscious awareness of God.

246

I get most of my knowledge in the night to use in the day. This is depicted in my little book called *YOUR DAY AND NIGHT*. The *INVOCATION FOR THE NIGHT* is a preparation for the night, and *SALUTATION TO THE DAY* is a philosophy and a policy upon which I endeavor to build my day.

* * *

Q. *How can one do this when one is unconscious in sleep?*

A. There is no such thing as a state of unconsciousness. People who go to sleep think they are unconscious because they stop thinking. Their electrical awareness of their body ceases, but their conscious or cosmic awareness is thoroughly alive. Very few of us have cosmic *awareness* in the night even though we often experience cosmic illumination, which we fail to recall upon awakening.

Desire what you will when you go to sleep, and you will have it. But also desire that you will retain it and remember it in the morning; and that desire will be answered, too. You will gradually develop the power of remembering your newly acquired knowledge.

The inspiration you get in the night, you carry into effect during the day. You will do ten times as much that day as you did the day before. You will have gained for your day that which has been given to you in the night. This is one of the secrets of multiplying one's power.

*   *   *

Q. *Do you consider yourself the messenger promised in all the holy books for this time?*

A. No! I consider everyone on earth a messenger, whether he runs an elevator or is president of a country. We are all messengers but I have been given a special message for man of this new age—and have been prepared for that message all my life since I was seven years of age. This preparation allowed me to go "behind the scenes" of the cosmic drama to see what it is all about. This experience gave me a state of knowledge which must now be unfolded.

*   *   *

Q. *In relation to the one great law of balance, will you please tell me if the crash of "the fall of man," as given in Genesis, caused the tipping of the earth's axis?*

A. No! The tipping of the earth's axis is a periodical thing which is happening as the earth gradually turns upside down. It is called the precession of the equinoxes in which the axis of the earth, which points north, forms a little circle around the heavens approximately every 2500 years. When the pyramids were built, a small tunnel was made pointing to the North Star; but if you look through the tunnel now, you will not see that same star because the axis of the earth has tipped. The pyramid is presumably 3000 years old. The North Star, which that tunnel then pointed to, has passed that same point once since that time, and will again pass it in about 1800 years.

When the earth was born on the equator of the sun, the axis of the earth did not tip. It was ninety degrees from the plane of the equator of the sun and parallel to the solar axis, as Mercury now is, and as all of the planets are when newly born from the sun. Planets are born from the sun by the way of rings sent out from the sun's equator—great nebulous rings which wind up upon themselves to become planets of the sun, just as the rings of Saturn will wind themselves up into moons. All of the moons of Saturn were rings. All of the moons of any satellite were first equatorial rings; then they became moons of the planet from which they were born. These moons in turn become comets when their orbits are sufficiently removed from their parent source.

Eventually everything which leaves the sun returns to it in various forms. This is as true of the rose in your garden as of the earth itself. All were born from the sun and must return to the sun for rebirth.

*   *   *

Q. *Do the electrons of our chemical elements turn as the axis of our earth and outer planets turn?*

A. Yes! All of them do except the electrons of one element which is known as carbon. All of carbon's electrons rotate upon the plane of their common equator, which is also the plane of their spherical nucleus.

That equator corresponds with the amplitude of the octave wave upon which carbon is born. It is the one element of the octave wave which is so perfectly in balance that it crystallizes as a true cube. The reason for this fact is because carbon rotates on one gyroscopic plane ninety degrees from its axis. All of the other elements rotate gyroscopically in planes of lesser and varying angles, as the planets and moons of our solar system do. The axis of electrons which thus vary must, likewise, turn in circles just as our outer planets do.

* * *

Q. *Are there any giant astronomical systems which are like carbon atoms?*

A. Yes! Many of them. Those that are the shape of a disc, seen edgewise, with a white hot sun in the middle, are like carbon atoms. You can see an excellent example of this type in *THE SECRET OF LIGHT*.

* * *

Q. *Are there any which are throwing off equatorial rings, as Saturn is doing?*

A. Yes! Thousands of them. The great nebula in

Lyra is such a one. Its one ring is millions of times larger than our whole solar system. In its center is a sun which was once a part of that giant ring. This central sun will keep throwing off rings until there is nothing left of it. That is the way suns turn inside out to become vacuous black holes instead of compressed incandescent solids. You will see a picture of the Lyra nebula in *THE SECRET OF LIGHT*.

*   *   *

Q. *You speak of other moons than ours. Do any of the other planets have a moon?*

A. Yes! All of the outer planets have more than one moon. Saturn and Jupiter have nine or ten each. Mars has two, for Mars is older than Earth. One of her moons, Phobos, is so newly born that it runs around its mother three times a day. Every seven and a half hours it completely encircles its mother; while Deimos, its older brother, takes four times as long.

The two inner planets, Mercury and Venus, have no moon children, for they are not yet old enough to have them.

*   *   *

Q. *You refer to moons as children of planets and of planets as their mothers. Are you speaking figuratively or literally?*

A. I am speaking literally. Planets are children of the sun who cannot have children of their own until they are old enough, just as children of men and women cannot have other children during their early childhood. Moons are children of planets, and comets are children of moons which, likewise, must grow quite old before they can have children.

You will note that the outer older planets have more children than the inner ones. Also the planets farthest out have lost some of their moons.

* * *

Q. *You speak of Mercury and Venus as not being old enough to have moon children. What is the condition they must arrive at to make them have children?*

A. Newly born children of the sun are very hot, and they are all mineral. There is no water on them, hence there can be no radiating vapors to help form equatorial rings. When water comes upon a planet, oxygen also comes. The coming of water, with its oxygen, is like the coming of puberty to humans.

A planet has not reached full maturity until mineral, vegetable and animal kingdoms have become possible upon it. The interchange between these three, with the waters of heavens and earth, makes the radiations of substantial rings imperative.

* * *

Q. *Why can we not see the moons of Mars, Jupiter and Saturn?*

A. Because they are too small and too far away

252

to be seen with the naked eye. We can easily see four of Jupiter's inner moons with a very low powered glass.

* * *

Q. *You said that we die when we breathe out and are reborn every time we breathe in. What do you mean by that?*

A. The whole purpose of breathing in is to recharge the body—to breathe out is to discharge it. We breathe in to live and breathe out to die.

The breathing process manifests the electric interchanging principle by means of which all things in earth and heaven appear, that they may forever disappear and reappear. We die every night and are reborn every morning when we awaken. Even the particles of matter which leave our body die to be reborn as new cells. Nature is forever repeating itself in every effect of motion, and in every patterned form.

* * *

Q. *Please explain this further.*

A. The particles of our body are dying all the time. A dog can follow us through the forest for days after we have passed because of the parts of our bodies which we have left behind. We are constantly restoring our bodies by life and death flowing through us—just as a spring of water is constantly replenished by water flowing into it and depleted by water flowing out of it. Breathing is the generating, degenerating and regenerating principle. We breathe in that we may be reborn. We eat food that we may replace that which has gone out of us in emanations of light. That which we take in as food to recharge our electric bodies creates new cells. Our breath is like a pump which pumps new cells into our bodies and pumps old cells out.

If we did not thus die continually, our bodies would weigh many tons. Life and death flow through us continually, each going opposite ways.

* * *

Q. *How can an infant born with an hereditary affliction be healed?*

A. The "sins" of the fathers and mothers are visited upon the children for generations. In any expression of life, a hereditary trait is due to a malformation of some kind, caused by wrong thinking or wrong action. We build our bodies by positive thought and action, and destroy them by negative thought and action. A disease may wreck the pattern of a body in part. The record of that changed pattern is stored in the seed to beget its kind.

* * *

Q. *Why should an innocent child be punished by deformity, or have to pay for a father's sins?*

A. The seed can only reproduce the pattern registered within it. A child is the extension of its forebears. Its body conforms to their patterns.

Any unbalance or imperfection in the pattern of the man-idea, the oak-tree idea, or any other patterned form, will correct itself after many rebirths. In Bar Harbor, for instance, pine trees growing on the edge of the sea cliffs are not like the pine trees growing five miles back from the sea. Those on the cliffs are rugged because of heavy winds. Their masses of foliage are closely knitted together at the top and their trunks are more staunch.

The trees look as though they have been bracing themselves against the winds for hundreds of centuries. They have fought the wind and the cold so long that their bark is stronger, their wood more dense. Their potential strength is greater because they have fought the winds so long. The pattern of all their fighting is in their seed, and the seed reproduces in kind. If you take that seed five miles inland, it will grow that kind of tree for perhaps ten generations, but gradually it will be like the tree that grows inland because it does not need to fight the winds any more.

V

QUESTIONS ANSWERED

Q. *What changes may we expect within the next seven years you have mentioned?*

A. The awareness of the nature of God is going to seep through this world during the next seven years. The love principle of *giving* which dominates the God-Mind will rule the world in the coming new age instead of the hate principle of *taking*. Man is finding that seed sown through his practice of taking is reaped in the harvest of fear and hate from which all crime springs.

We are going to find that the practice of the love principle gives us intense happiness and a power that we never dreamed of before. Gradually we shall be able to keep our doors unlocked, for we shall no longer fear our neighbor. The practice of the love principle is creeping into the world, and by 1953 we shall see much of the effects of it in our civilization. When love comes into the world, fear and hate disappear.

The two greatest elements of society today are religion and science. We cannot get along without either of them. They are our very fundamentals. We are going to see a marriage between religion and science. We are going to see their present disunity replaced by unity. Gradually a new world will come out of science. Science will no longer say, "We can get along with just the lever of motion. We do not need to know there is a fulcrum under the lever."

We are going to find that science will verify God. Knowledge of the nature of God will come through science, not through religion.

Our world of today is a different kind of world from that of even one hundred years ago. Our world of radar, television and electricity has given mankind a different conception of the universe. Out of our new conception of natural law, a greater comprehension of our electric universe of light-waves is being born. The race of man will be uplifted in accordance with its ability to comprehend the nature of our universe and its Creator.

* * *

Q. *When you use the expression, "Knowing versus thinking," do you mean something akin to what is ordinarily meant by "Intuition versus reasoning?"*

A. Intuition or inspiration is the still small Voice of our *knowing*. First we faintly recognize an inner whispering that we *know* to be *truth*. This we call intuition. It may take form in an inspirational idea.

When we faithfully follow the idea and meet with success, we learn the wisdom of following our intuitions and gradually the Inner Voice gains strength.

Thinking is taking knowledge of the whole idea apart and setting it in motion as many separate ideas.

Reasoning is coordinating a group of thoughts and is purely objective.

Knowing is that which is the Light within us. It is the *cause* of the *effect* which our senses observe.

* * *

Q. *When one prays, to whom does he pray?*

A. One prays directly to God—not through any person or thing. There is only God and His Creation. God created this universe. You are part of His universe. You extend directly from God as one with Him in His Light. He is the *only* Source of your power. Your direct connection with your Creator is through the centering Consciousness within yourself. You talk to God when you commune with that Self which is within you. God and the centering Self are One.

* * *

Q. *How can one make God friendly rather than an awesome something?*

A. People think of God as awesome simply because they think of some unknown Being sternly ruling us from somewhere far away. One must *know* that God is omnipresent and centers everyone. The still Light of Love not only centers the Consciousness of everyone, but also centers every cell in one's body and in the whole universe. One loses the idea of awesomeness by companionship, because one then feels the ever-present God of love.

When you first meet a man like Thomas Edison, you are awed by him because you realize you are in the presence of a man who is a vastly superior person. But after awhile, the humility and the friendliness of such a man as Edison—who does not think of himself as being superior—make you lose all sense of awesomeness.

* * *

Q. *How do you think spiritual and material science can best be united to serve the welfare of humanity, and raise the standard of living for all?*

A. It can best be united by getting rid of the disunity in both. Science is material; it is concerned only with effect, and that is why it has so little knowledge. It says, "We are not interested in anything we cannot prove in the laboratory."

God cannot be proven in the laboratory because that which you can prove in the laboratory is limited to matter and motion—to effect of cause—but in every laboratory experiment there is always a third unexplainable quality which is necessary to produce the effect. That third quality is the equilibrium of *cause* from which *effect* springs.

Science seeks *cause* of all things in the matter and motion it alone deals in. It seeks the cause of energy in motion and the life principle in germs, which are also matter in motion. It must eventually find that *cause* lies in the stillness of the One Light from which the electric universe of motion springs.

Science has found radar and other heretofore unknown phenomena. I have full confidence that science will eventually verify God. *When science at last verifies God, the hundreds of primitive doctrinal religions will topple, and a new race will arise from that wreckage.*

God, the Creator, is a scientific fact. His Creation is a material manifestation of that scientific fact. In order to know the nature of God, we must have a scientific foundation for our metaphysics instead of an abstract one.

I repeat, when we at last comprehend the nature of the universe and live the law of cosmic love, the standards of living must be high—and beautiful—because love can only bring happiness through the interchange of all things—material, mental and spiritual.

* * *

Q. *Please explain karma as you understand it.*

A. As I understand it, karma means that whatever you do is electrically recorded in your seed for eternal repetition in kind. When you break the law, the law breaks you to an equal extent at that precise moment—not the next moment. It starts immediately, even if it takes generations to void it. You are in balance or you are out of it. If you are out of balance with the universe, you have to get back into balance.

Nature demands balance. Karma is an evidence of unbalance which must eventually be voided by balance.

* * *

Q. *How would the law of karma apply to a suicide?*

A. Suicide is an evidence of fear and weakness. A suicide is afraid to face life, or to endure its real or fancied hardships.

That weakness must eventually be balanced by acquiring strength, even if it takes a hundred reincarnations. The suicide has not escaped anything by ending his life. He has but delayed his own unfoldment.

* * *

Q. *Please explain again your instruction of how you prepare for the night; also that plan of yours for going to sleep when thoughts hold you awake.*

A. If one decentrates, electric thought-waves expand and thinking ceases. This is the condition needed for sleep. It is the condition where the brain refuses to form thought patterns.

I find that I can decentrate better by imagining a black hole. If thought patterns still persist in forming, I thrust them down that formless black hole. Very soon I go to sleep.

In preparing to acquire cosmic knowledge during the night, the important thing is to forget the body. It is easier to forget the body when it is in a comfortable position and not over-stimulated by too much eating and drinking.

The senses are only aware of motion; they are not aware of stillness or of balance. *You cannot sense the fact that you are comfortable. You can only know that you are comfortable.* If your body is cold, your senses will react to warn your nerves which electrically inform you it is cold. If you put on an overcoat or a blanket, you become warm. Your senses then stop vibrating.

A musician could not compose a symphony if someone were scratching him with a pin, making him aware of his body. Neither can you become in tune with the Infinite while being tormented by a sensed awareness of your body.

When thus in tune, write your desire in the pulse-beat of the universe, which is your own pulse-beat. You are then in the universe of *knowing,* and your desire for cosmic knowledge will be answered.

The difficulty is to recollect it when you awaken.

Even when you do recollect it, you often negate it by doubting or fearing to put it into effect.

*   *   *

Q. *Can one ask for good paying work—for guidance as to how much to ask for it—and where to go for it?*

A. Of course you can! You must have implicit confidence in yourself. If you are qualified to do certain things and have sufficient confidence in yourself, you should be able to set a fair value upon your services. If you do not have confidence and underrate your ability, you pull yourself down. Overconfidence—too much ego—asking too much for services—will lead to failure.

I will give you an example of what I mean: A major, who had been in the war from the beginning, came back and said to me, "I have the greatest worry in the world. I am fifty-four years of age. I had a position, when I went away, in which I got seventy-five hundred a year. Now I am older and feel that if I go back to the same place, they will take me out to lunch, treat me nicely, of course, and perhaps put me on their list or something. I feel insecure and very worried. What shall I do about it?"

I said, "You go back to that place without any such negative thoughts in your head. Say to them, 'Gentlemen, I have given much thought to coming

263

back with you, but I have acquired much valuable experience in these past years, and know that I would be of greater value to you now. If you want me back I will come, but not for seventy-five hundred a year. Make it fifteen thousand and I will come.' "

He did that and they gave him a contract for fifteen thousand dollars a year. You see, he had manufactured that worry and trouble for himself. He had made up his mind that he could not go back to his old job. We must never underestimate ourselves, for if we do we shall reflect our negative thinking in everyone we contact. Neither must we negate our desires by doubts.

VI

QUESTIONS ANSWERED

Q. *When I was about ten years old, I heard God call me on two different occasions, but did not do as He asked me. Have been trying for some time to hear Him again, but without any success. I wonder why?*

A. It may be that you are not alone often enough to commune with God. It is impossible to have that experience without its constant recurrence if you deeply desire it.

*　　*　　*

Q. *Please define: "The music of the spheres."*

A. That is really a poetic phrase, but it has reality back of it because this is a wave universe. Waves of light have all effects in them—including sound.

Celestial spheres are always in motion, and they send out wave vibrations of light pressures all through the universe. When waves vibrate, sound extends from them. If one's ears were attuned to those wave vibrations, one would hear the sounds of them, but the ears of the body are not so attuned. The beauty of the universe of stars appeals to the eyes of the Spirit, and Inner Ears hear those mighty rhythms.

Consider the music of the sphere you are upon. Waves of the ocean issue a sound which your ears can hear. The breeze through the trees also issues sounds that your ears can hear. Each sound is the same tone in the octave, although the character of the sounds of water crashing on the sand differs from the sounds of wind coming through the trees. Each planet and star has a tone of its own, just as each string of a harp has a tone of its own.

"F" is our earth tone and wherever you hear the music of this sphere the tone is "F." Ocean waves crashing upon the shores of a distant planet, or electric storms on suns, are too distant to reach you, but they are there just the same even if your ears cannot hear them.

The sound of a voice cannot be heard very far without an amplifier or a radio, but you know it goes all over the earth. You can condense it anywhere and the sound can be repeated there. All sound is universal. It extends to every sphere and is repeated in every one. The reason for this is that all matter simulates light, and so do all waves. All spheres are mirrors of light which reflect all other light.

The radio is just an echo of the sounds which are mirrored from somewhere else; just as the voice hits on a cliff side, re-condenses and reflects as an echo.

Every action in the universe extends into the farthest reaches of space and is echoed upon every star in the universe. The chirp of a cricket on earth will echo against the surface of distant Arcturus. Naturally one cannot hear it, but it is there. That is the scientific explanation of the poetic phrase "The music of the spheres."

* * *

Q. *I have the creative type of mind. From my childhood I have always known the spiritual ecstasy of which you speak. The world has not been ready for what I had to give; it is ready now and I am past seventy-five. I long to give it but have a frail body. You say I have no limitations; therefore, rejuvenation is possible. Any words of encouragement would be acceptable.*

A. Desire is the basis of all things and all Creation. That which you mentally desire to do, you can do at any age. Sir Walter Scott wrote all of his books after he was forty. If you are physically unable to express your thoughts by lecturing or teaching, you can still write or dictate. You, too, can be one of the messengers who uplift mankind if you *live* your principles. By living them, you extend them to all others. By living them dynamically you, yourself, are the seed of your principles. Seed planted in good ground will grow and spread. The planting of a seed anywhere within the limitations of your physical capacity will spread all around the planet. Nothing can stop it. That feeling of ecstasy in a man sitting upon a mount, knowing that God is within him, uplifts all mankind.

If the greatest musician kept his ecstasy to himself, the world would not be enriched by it because he would not have planted the seed of his idea in other minds. His inspiration would end where it began—so it could never reinspire another with his ecstasy.

There is always some way within the limitations of one's physical condition to reinspire others with one's own immortality by giving that immortality to them, if only to two or three in your immediate midst. That will make you younger—it will make you stronger. The ecstasy of that alone will give power to your body by giving it balance. Ecstatic man is vital, no matter if he is twenty or a hundred.

Dan Beard was ninety-two when I made a bust of him and he was very vital in mind and action. It is always a wrong idea to think that we grow feeble of mind as we grow older. We may grow feeble in body—yes!—that is natural. But one's Consciousness should be keener every day of one's life until the last minute.

* * *

Q. *If one desires greatly to help someone at a distance, what method should be used?*

A. To help one at a distance, the most direct and best method to use is by letter, telegram and mental desire to extend your balance and power to the one who needs it. Telepathy is direct, but we have not yet reached the point in our unfoldment where we can use our telepathetic powers effectively.

Everyone in the universe is connected by an invisible electric cable, but we have not yet unfolded sufficiently to that stage of awareness which allows us to make practical use of it. Prayer, or desire, extend you to another through the omnipotent Light of God which centers all of us. The more we are aware of that Light, the more we can make use of it; but mankind as a whole is still barbarian and has but little comprehension of that Light.

* * *

Q. *How can we develop our spiritual power?*

A. Comprehension will do that—comprehension of the nature of God and His universe, and of our relation to it. Understanding of our electric unity as far as bodies are concerned—and knowledge of our spiritual unity in the one Light—will gradually give us that power.

* * *

Q. *I know that the wonderful freedom of easy breathing, just as the keenness of senses of sight, hearing, etc., is closely associated with "inner feel-*

ing." Is there any simple rule that might be applied to bring about this ease?

A. There is a technique of breathing that is practiced by Hindus a great deal, and even by athletes. It is a technique that is physical—being connected with the senses of the body. One has to be aware of the body to cultivate such a breathing technique.

In order to cultivate cosmic illumination, one must get rid of the awareness of body sensing to find the stillness of the God-Light. Anything which ties one to the physical is a detriment to freeing oneself from it in order to make the transition into the spiritual universe.

A man once told me that he walked up and down the street, or his room, to induce inspiration. The repetitive rhythm of walking up and down the street induced this ecstasy of inner feeling in him. That man's desire demanded some sort of action of his body, but the more he repeated the action rhythmically, the more automatic the action became. If one automatically repeats any action long enough, he gradually becomes unaware that he is doing it. It becomes a body habit, like the beating of his heart. This habit-forming process consumes a lot of unnecessary time. Breathing techniques fall into this class of time-consuming formula where action is required to attain stillness.

Q. *Will there be a depression before 1953?*

A. We are heading that way. There will be one unless it is averted by changing the present conditions. Something may be rolling downhill, but if it runs against a stump, it stops rolling. We are now rolling downhill through disharmony and disunity. We are still sowing and reaping the harvest of the war that we have just been through. Unless we find balance between labor and management, and the law of rhythmic balanced interchange is established in every branch of industrial, commercial and governmental human relations, we shall have a depression in the midst of plenty.

We need millions of houses but cannot produce them because of unbalanced conditions. All down the economic line, unbalanced conditions are creating havoc. Until balance is restored, we cannot have the normalcy we require for a stabilized economy.

* * *

Q. *You have said, "There is One Thinker." What is it then that we call the senses?*

A. The One Thinker is God, and when you think, you are creating with the Creator; you are actually a co-Creator with Him. Animals do not think; they sense. When we have reached the point where we are aware of God in us, we are knowing with God as well as sensing with the body. *Knowing* is expressed by thinking. *Knowing* is cosmic—thinking is electric. Thinking produces electric action through the senses.

The senses are merely the nerves which wire all parts of the body machine together so that they act when called upon. The senses of man do not think any more than the wires of a machine think.

* * *

Q. *Henry George in his book, "Progress and Poverty," contends that capital comes from labor and that labor and capital in essence are the same. Please comment.*

A. Capital and labor are opposites. Every idea of everything in Nature is divided into pairs of opposites, and these opposites interchange. They are opposite conditions of the same thing in every case and they always oppose. If they did not oppose, there could be no transaction between the two.

Compression is the opposite of expansion. Expansion pushes outward radially; compression pushes inward radially. The interchange between these two unbalanced conditions voids them both. Each then becomes the other, as all opposites in Nature must do.

Capital and labor interchange. Capital alone could not produce without labor; labor assists it to produce. They interchange their opposition and thus void their opposition. Labor thus receives money from capital so that the laborer can become the capitalist and reinvest that money in something that he desires. Capital is thus enabled to produce again from what it received from labor, and labor is enabled to purchase again with the money it receives from capital.

In truth, they are one through continual interchange, as the moving pendulum is one even though it swings two ways. There is a constant cycle of interchange between all opposites. Compression eternally interchanges with expansion in order to produce motion. Life and death interchange day by day—moment by moment—to simulate eternal life by eternal repetition of opposed interchanging.

* * *

Q. *What is the difference between magnetism and electricity?*

A. Magnetism is the word used by science on the supposition that it is a force which attracts—picks up needles and certain metals. That effect is an illusion of the senses. Magnetism is the still Light of God which centers everything as its equilibrium. Wherever you can locate the source of magnetic light, you locate a position where God is in evidence —as in the magnetic poles or the center of gravity of the earth—or the sun—or the center of a shaft in an engine.

All power and force is in the stillness of the center, but the power and force are manifested by motion around the center. The center never moves, but is all power. It is the vortex of electric whirlpools which we call cyclones. It centers the positive and negative parts of a wave as the wave fulcrum. Matter is wound up into dense spheres and unwound into space surrounding those spheres. It is wound up via the poles and unwound via the equator. The winding process is electric and the vortex at the poles manifests the cyclone principle.

When a cyclone picks up houses and trees and dashes them around, that is electric power expressed by motion. Electricity is motion entirely—positive and negative forces in opposition. Electricity is tearing up the houses—the cyclone of electricity—not magnetism. The center of the cyclone is so still that not a blade of grass moves, even when the winds around it are 180 miles an hour. That still point is the omnipresent Light where God is located, centering it to extend power for expressing cyclonic motion. Motion and matter have no power in themselves. The still Light is the fulcrum on which the electric wave lever moves.

Electricity is merely the servant of Mind. The electric servant does what it is willed to do. It builds the universe of matter as Mind directs. Matter cannot move without being willed to move by the desire of Mind. Even your little finger cannot move without your Mind willing it to move.

Q. *You say the Light of God is still, absolutely still, with no activity whatsoever. We are taught by the recognized metaphysical authorities, who have been teaching for years, that in the God-Mind is all activity of very high vibrations of the spirit which gradually slow down as matter becomes more dense —until in solid matter, like granite, they are very slow. Which teaching are we to believe?*

A. Metaphysicians talk about "getting into the stillness—or silence." The Bible says: "Be still and know." It is illogical to talk of getting into the high vibrations to seek stillness since vibrations mean motion and high vibrations mean intense motion.

I do not know who told the metaphysicians what they are teaching, but that teaching is not true of God's law. It is certain that such teachings could not have come from science, for science fully recognizes the fact that vibration frequencies multiply in the direction of density. That fact is the step-up-transformer principle of Nature.

The God-Mind of the One Light could not be active. It is absolutely still, absolutely vibrationless. Matter alone vibrates. The more dense the matter, the greater the vibration. Activity or vibration means an oscillation between two opposite conditions. There cannot be two opposite conditions in the One Light of God. If that were so, the unchanging God would be forever changing. Between two cells of a battery there is an equilibrium. That equilibrium is halfway between the positive and negative poles.

Consider a bar magnet. You see a positive pole on one end and a negative pole on the other. The positive and negative poles will pick up nails because they are active, changing and conditioned with electric power; but they are centered by still magnetic Light. The activity expressed at the ends is borrowed from the stillness of the equilibrium which centers them. The principle of the fulcrum and lever applies here as it does to all vibrating waves. All of the power expressed by the moving lever is in the fulcrum. The fulcrum *never* moves. The lever *always* moves.

*　　*　　*

Q. *How can one learn to relax to find cosmic Consciousness?*

A. One must lose one's individuality in order to find the Self which centers one—the Consciousness of the God-Self which centers all things. One then finds universal Consciousness. One can then work knowingly with God and double, treble or quadruple one's capacity for creative expression. God-Consciousness is more easily attained in solitary aloneness when the whisperings of the Inner Voice can be heard with the ears of the Soul.

VII

QUESTIONS ANSWERED

Q. *Can one treat a person who disbelieves in the truths of healing, who though only about fifty years of age, considers life not worth living and is emotionally and physically ill? If so how?*

A. The only way that can be done is through desire. Desire is the basis and foundation of the universe. If a man is without desire, he cannot successfully surmount the hurdles of life. Desire is an ever-flowing fountain. Stop desiring and the ever-flowing fountain of man's power ceases. The person who lacks desire will eventually destroy himself. Nature preserves only that which it has use for in carrying out its purposes. We are manifesting Creation by being creators. We cannot be creators unless we desire to be, and the greater our desire for purposeful expression, the greater the power for manifesting our Creator.

Lacking that desire, Nature creates toxins to destroy all purposeless things. All life is expressed by a series of waves. The positive electric side of a wave is alkaline. All alkaline elements wind up tight; they

277

compress into solids by thrusting inward from without, and they continue that in an octave of one, two, three, four, until they get to carbon, which has the highest melting point of any element, thirty-five hundred degrees centigrade.

The moment they pass the amplitude of the wave and start unwinding down its acid side, they begin to expand to tear carbon apart into nitrogen, oxygen and fluorine negative gases.

The amplitude of a wave is its crest. It is the highest point of desire in the octaves of the elements, or in the cycle of your life. It is the maturing point of greatest strength, as a man of forty is "in his prime."

If you then begin to lose your desire, you also begin to lose your power, as carbon does when it is unwound into negative gases instead of positive solids.

We can take a lesson from the elements of Nature in relation to our own expression of life. When our desires remain positive, we reach the strength of our amplitude, which we refer to as "being on the crest of the wave." When our desires become negative, we express weakness. It is then that self-pity, self-condemnation, pessimism, inferiority complexes and excuses pull us down to the depths of despair.

This negation of desire is the easy road to failure and ruin. Only deep positive and constructive desires can again lift us up and back to the crest of our wave.

*   *   *

Q. *Is that the reason why men are apt to soon die when they retire from active life at middle age?*

A. That is often the reason because with retirement comes a lack of desire for creative expression. If one retires to take it easy, just to live life without purpose, Nature gets rid of such useless bodies, for Nature is purposeful. She gives purposeful things long life and strength to manifest her purposes.

If, on the other hand, a man retires at middle-age to engage in some other purposeful pursuit which keeps positive desire alive and strong in him, Nature will not eliminate him. That is why mentally-alert positive thinkers remain vital until their very last days of a ripe old age.

*   *   *

Q. *What relation have toxins to what you have been telling us about?*

A. Toxins develop to destroy any organic body which has become out of balance in any one of the many ways unbalance is created. Fear, hate and anger develop destructive toxins in one's body; for fear, hate and anger have no place in Nature. This is a universe of love. The purpose of the Creator is to express love only by giving love.

279

When one hates, or fears, or is angry, one is working against the purposefulness of Nature. Nature begins his destruction by giving him self-manufactured toxic poison in an amount equal to the fear, hate or anger he has given out of himself.

Cancers and many other forms of organic diseases arise in the body from these self-inflicted poisons. These will continue so long as their cause continues. If the cause is removed by replacing it with love, the body will clear itself of its toxic poisons by the flow of love through it, just as a spring of water will clear itself of mud thrown into it by clear crystal water flowing through it.

If, however, mud is continued to be thrown into the spring, it will never clear. Likewise, people who continue to throw hate into their blood streams can never be well until they clarify their whole organisms with the flow of love to balance all their unbalanced conditions.

* * *

Q. *Do you think an artist should aim to create objects which will sell, or create what he likes himself —even though the public may not care for them?*

A. It is an artist's first duty to manifest God. His emotions or inspirations should express the Self within him. The genius will express his spiritual Self regardless of material return. He who exploits his genius will lose it.

George Gershwin varied intensely from the traditional classic music of Wagner, Beethoven, Mozart or Chopin. When he first began to compose, he was heartily condemned because his music was not in line of tradition. But he gave the world a new idea. He gave it an idea in motive and rhythm which uplifted it; but it was strongly physical as well as spiritual. The music of Wagner can make you absolutely forget the body and bring you into the presence of the Divine within yourself.

George Gershwin's music did that, also, but it made you feel aware of the life and power flowing through your body because he syncopated the Universal tones to some extent, but he kept motive, rhythm, law and order in his music. So who is to condemn a person for creating that which he, himself, desires to create, whether he breaks tradition or not? If at first one cannot turn one's art into money, find money some other way, but never sacrifice one's ideals for money.

*   *   *

Q. *What would you say is one of the most vital principles of The Message of The Divine Iliad to bring about world peace?*

A. I believe you have heard me state over and over again that Balance was the most vital word given to me in my illumination twenty-five years ago. In its fullness, that vital principle was given as *Rhythmic Balanced Interchange.*

What man must learn and practice if he would know and hold peace is the art of giving. *"All that ye give shall be given back a hundredfold."* This is God's law. If we give, we must receive because we then become a vacuum which must be filled.

The Message of The Divine Iliad gives scientific explanation of all of Nature's processes in lucid and simple language.

Man could not know anything but peace and happiness if he understood and lived the Universal Law of Love which gives all for regiving. I repeat that the Law of Love is fully expressed in the three words, *Rhythmic Balanced Interchange.*

* * *

Q. *Is the "Secret of Light" intended for those trained in the field of science?*

A. No! It is intended for comprehension of all people. It has taken twenty-five years for me to learn how to write the "Secret of Light" in language everybody could understand. The first rehearsal of it was called "The Universal One." In that book were all my chemical charts, even the elements that constitute the atom bomb. However, the presentation was too complex and involved to be understood.

The simple story of Creation is the hardest story to tell. I went through all the throes of learning the terminology of science because in my cosmic training no terms were used. The heartbeat of the universe was the basis of my knowledge of how God puts His electric universe together and takes it apart again.

That pulse beat is the basis of the octave wave. In it lies the secret of Creation. One could teach music, chemistry, or all the sciences from it because it is the basis of them all. It is the sex principle of the universe which is registered in your heartbeat. The pulse beat of the universe is divided into zero, one, two, three, four—four, three, two, one, zero. The octaves of the elements are founded upon these pressure divisions as, also, is the spectrum of light. The whole structure of human life is founded upon the basic two-way sex principle.

*   *   *

Q. *What parts do a husband and child play in the life of a woman of genius? Is the woman genius handicapped by them?*

A. Every experience in life multiplies the power of a genius to express life. The child and the husband contribute to her self expression, no matter what the conditions are around her. Nothing is an obstacle to genius. Genius knows no hurdles. A great genius must be worthy of this genius. That is what I mean by living life.

This woman genius should be thankful that she has a husband and child. She should succeed in spite of the time they take. She must work more. She must do all the things that a wife and mother should do, even to all the little tasks of bed making and dish washing. It all adds to the ability of one to express the rhythms of God's thinking. Whatever one is, is evidenced by what one creates.

*　　*　　*

Q. *Is the study of the life and teachings of Jesus a help in the unfoldment of Consciousness?*

A. Naturally, yes! Jesus is the greatest teacher that we have ever known, and it is a tremendous pity that He is not here today to tell the things He knew in the words that He could now use. Today He would not ask you to rely upon faith and belief, for we can now comprehend things which were beyond the comprehension of His day.

The teachings of Jesus are the foundation upon which we build, but we must have more comprehension of His teachings. He said: *"There are many things I could tell ye, but ye cannot bear them now."* He meant by that that the people of His time did not have the comprehension that the electric age has given us. It is through comprehension of Nature that the doors will open to the Light and give us a greater awareness of the Consciousness of the One Being within us.

* * *

Q. *What is your definition of prayer?*

A. I would say desire. We always pray because we desire something. Often people have asked me how I pray because it has often been said that I do not use words. That is not exactly true. If you read my little book, "Your Day and Night," you will find in it my prayer for the night in which I prepare my body to go to sleep. I write that desire upon my heart, and that prayer is a perfectly legal one. It asks God for nothing but what Mind and body needs to manifest God worthily.

The "Salutation to the Day" is my prayer for the day. It is a philosophy of life. I do not pray in words, for words consume time. When you *know* these prayers as a whole, you do not need the words—you need only the knowing. I translate everything I have to do from the universe of sensing to the universe of knowing, so that I know that idea as a whole; and when I go to bed at night, or when I awaken in the morning, I do not say these prayers in words because

I know them. When one knows anything as a whole concept, one does not need to take it apart and put it into words.

If you ask someone if he knows "Uncle Tom's Cabin," of course he knows it. He has seen it so often that he does not have to think it into parts. He knows it timelessly. I reduce all my desires, that may take one page or ten, into an essence of *knowing* when I go to sleep, and that knowing is my prayer. It is the desire written upon my heart as a wordless concept. That is the policy which I carry through my day and try to live.

* * *

Q. *If death goes toward life and life goes toward death in a balanced interchange, could one not live on indefinitely—or at least dispense with the disintegration called old age?*

A. No. If life interchanges with death, that means that life is giving itself to death and death to life. In other words, life and death continually void each other. Life integrates and death disintegrates. Each becomes the other alternately. Each is one-half of a cycle. Cycles cannot continue indefinitely, but they must be forever repeated sequentially.